Characterization of Hydrology and Salinity in the Dolores Project Area, McElmo Creek Region, Southwest Colorado, Water Years 1978–2006

By Rodney J. Richards and Kenneth J. Leib

Prepared in cooperation with the Bureau of Reclamation and the Colorado River Salinity Control Forum

Scientific Investigations Report 2010–5218

U.S. Department of the Interior
U.S. Geological Survey

U.S. Department of the Interior
KEN SALAZAR, Secretary

U.S. Geological Survey
Marcia K. McNutt, Director

U.S. Geological Survey, Reston, Virginia: 2011

For more information on the USGS—the Federal source for science about the Earth, its natural and living resources, natural hazards, and the environment, visit http://www.usgs.gov or call 1-888-ASK-USGS

For an overview of USGS information products, including maps, imagery, and publications, visit http://www.usgs.gov/pubprod

To order this and other USGS information products, visit http://store.usgs.gov

Suggested citation:
Richards, R.J., and Leib, K.J., 2011, Characterization of hydrology and salinity in the Dolores project area, McElmo Creek Region, southwest Colorado, 1978–2006: U.S. Geological Survey Scientific Investigations Report 2010–5218, 38 p.

Contents

Figures

Tables

Conversion Factors

Inch/Pound to SI

Multiply	By	To obtain
Length		
inch (in.)	2.54	centimeter (cm)
inch (in.)	25.4	millimeter (mm)
foot (ft)	0.3048	meter (m)
mile (mi)	1.609	kilometer (km)
mile, nautical (nmi)	1.852	kilometer (km)
yard (yd)	0.9144	meter (m)
Area		
acre	4,047	square meter (m^2)
acre	0.004047	square kilometer (km^2)
square mile (mi^2)	2.590	square kilometer (km^2)
Volume		
acre-foot (acre-ft)	1,233	cubic meter (m^3)
Flow rate		
acre-foot per year (acre-ft/yr)	0.001233	cubic hectometer per year (hm^3/yr)
cubic foot per second (ft^3/s)	0.02832	cubic meter per second (m^3/s)
Mass		
ton per day (ton/d)	0.9072	metric ton per day
ton per year (ton/yr)	0.9072	metric ton per year

Temperature in degrees Celsius (°C) may be converted to degrees Fahrenheit (°F) as follows:

$$°F=(1.8×°C)+32$$

Temperature in degrees Fahrenheit (°F) may be converted to degrees Celsius (°C) as follows:

$$°C=(°F-32)/1.8$$

Vertical coordinate information is referenced to the National Geodetic Vertical Datum of 1929 (NGVD 29).

Horizontal coordinate information is referenced to the North American Datum of 1983 (NAD 83).

Specific conductance is given in microsiemens per centimeter at 25 degrees Celsius (µS/cm at 25 °C).

Concentrations of chemical constituents in water are given either in milligrams per liter (mg/L) or micrograms per liter (µg/L).

Water year is defined in this report as the 12-month period October 1 through September 30, designated by the calendar year in which it ends.

Acronyms

USGS   U.S. Geological Survey
USBR   Bureau of Reclamation
NRCS   Natural Resources Conservation Service
CDWR   Colorado Division of Water Resources
CRSCF   Colorado River Salinity Control Forum

Characterization of Hydrology and Salinity in the Dolores Project Area, McElmo Creek Region, Southwest Colorado, Water Years 1978–2006

By Rodney J. Richards and Kenneth J. Leib

Abstract

Increasing salinity loading in the Colorado River has become a major concern for agricultural and municipal water supplies. The Colorado Salinity Control Act was implemented in 1974 to protect and enhance the quality of water in the Colorado River Basin. The U.S. Geological Survey, in cooperation with the Bureau of Reclamation and the Colorado River Salinity Control Forum, summarized salinity reductions in the McElmo Creek basin in southwest Colorado as a result of salinity-control modifications and flow-regime changes that result from the Dolores Project, which consists of the construction of McPhee reservoir on the Dolores River and salinity control modifications along the irrigation water delivery system.

Flow-adjusted salinity trends using S-LOADEST estimations for a streamgage on McElmo Creek (site 1), that represents outflow from the basin, indicates a decrease in salinity load by 39,800 tons from water year 1978 through water year 2006, which is an average decrease of 1,370 tons per year for the 29-year period. Annual-load calculations for a streamgage on Mud Creek (site 6), that represents outflow from a tributary basin, indicate a decrease of 7,300 tons from water year 1982 through water year 2006, which is an average decrease of 292 tons per year for the 25-year period. The streamgage Dolores River at Dolores, CO (site 17) was chosen to represent a background site that is not affected by the Dolores Project. Annual load calculations for site 17 estimated a decrease of about 8,600 tons from water year 1978 through water year 2006, which is an average decrease of 297 tons per year for the 29-year period. The trend in salinity load at site 17 was considered to be representative of a natural trend in the region.

Typically, salinity concentrations at outflow sites decreased from the pre-Dolores Project period (water years 1978–1984) to the post-Dolores Project period (water years 2000–2006). The median salinity concentration for site 1 (main basin outflow) decreased from 2,210 milligrams per liter per day in the preperiod to 2,110 milligrams per liter per day in the postperiod. The median salinity concentration for site 6 (tributary outflow) increased from 3,370 milligrams per liter per day in the preperiod to 3,710 milligrams per liter per day in the postperiod. Salinity concentrations typically increased at inflow sites from the preperiod to the postperiod. Salinity concentrations increased from 178 milligrams per liter per day during the preperiod at Main Canal #1 (site 16) to 227 milligrams per liter per day during the postperiod at the Dolores Tunnel Outlet near Dolores, CO (site 15).

Calculation of the historical flow regime in McElmo Creek was done using a water-budget analysis of the basin. During water years 2000–2006, an estimated 845,000 acre-feet of water was consumed by crops and did not return to the creek as streamflow. The remaining 76,000 acre-feet, or 10,900 acre-feet per year for the 7-year postperiod, was assumed to represent a historical flow condition. The historical flow of 10,900 acre-feet per year is equivalent to 15.1 cubic feet per second.

Average total dissolved solids concentrations for water in each type of sedimentary rock were used to estimate natural salinity loads. Most surface-water sites used to fit the criteria needed to achieve a natural TDS concentration were springs. An average spring TDS value for sandstones geology in the basin was 350 milligrams per liter, and the average value for Mancos Shale geology was 4,000 milligrams per liter. The natural salinity loads in McElmo Creek were estimated to be 29,100 tons per year, which is 43 percent of the salinity load that was calculated for the postperiod.

Introduction

The Colorado Salinity Control Act, Public Law 93–320, June 24, 1974, was enacted to enhance and protect the quality of water in the Colorado River. Title II of the Colorado Salinity Control Act authorized the investigation and implementation of control measures for selected salinity-control units, including the McElmo Creek basin in Montezuma County, southwestern Colorado (fig. 1) (Bureau of Reclamation, 2003). Salinity is a concern in the McElmo Creek region of the Upper Colorado River Basin. The development of McPhee Reservoir, which is fed by the Dolores River, as part of the Dolores Project in the early 1980s provided additional irrigation water for

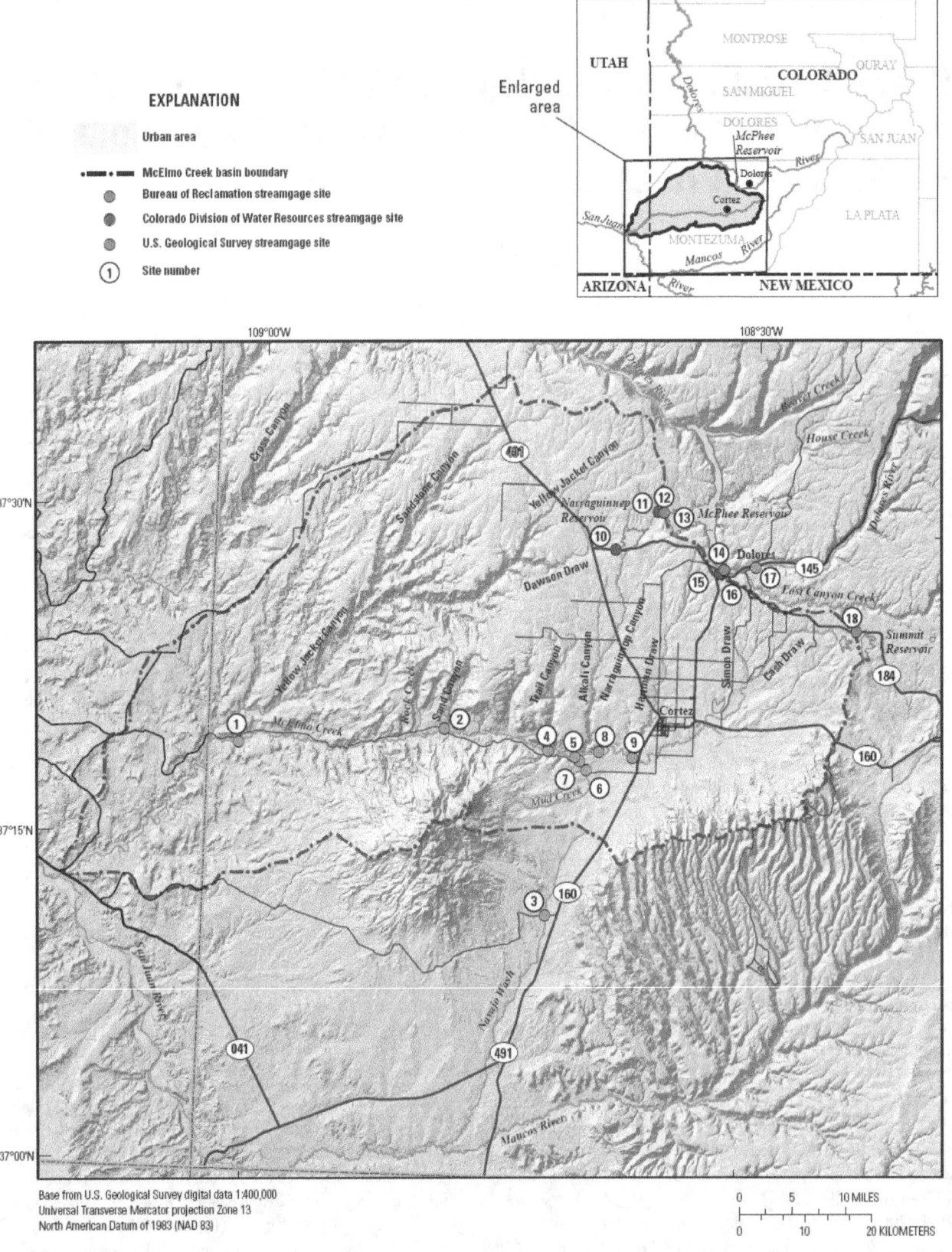

Figure 1.   Location of McElmo Creek basin and location of streamgage sites used in the analysis of salinity load.

the McElmo Creek basin and lengthened the irrigation season, which potentially allowed for increases in salinity to McElmo Creek and its tributaries (Bureau of Reclamation, 1988).

The term salinity is defined as a concentration of dissolved mineral salts and solids in water (Hem, 1959). Salinity is typically used synonymously with the terms salt or total dissolved solids (TDS). However, in this report, salinity refers to total dissolved solids in streams, whereas the term salt is used to describe mineral salts that have not been moved or transported to another location and remain in situ.

McElmo Creek basin has been identified as a major contributor of salinity from both irrigation and natural sources (fig. 1). The Bureau of Reclamation (USBR) estimates that 47 percent of the salinity load in the Colorado River Basin is derived from natural sources including geological formations, saline springs, and surface runoff (Bureau of Reclamation, 2003). Approximately 37 percent of the salinity load in the basin results from irrigation, and the remaining 16 percent results from reservoir-storage effects and municipal and industrial practices. Evaporation of exposed water and evapotranspiration by plants can result in the formation of mineral and salt deposits, which become dissolved as the deposits come in contact with water. Coastal and marine sedimentary rocks, such as those that occur in the study area, are substantial sources of mineral and salt deposits due to the evapoconcentration of saline waters during the time of deposition. Irrigation water can dissolve near-surface salt deposits through canal seepage and percolation beyond the lower limits of the root zone into groundwater (deep percolation). The concentrated base flow returns to the stream either as surface water or groundwater, increasing the salinity load in the Colorado River and tributaries to the Colorado River (Iorns and others, 1965).

Salinity-control projects such as irrigation and water-delivery system improvements have been implemented in the McElmo Creek basin to reduce the overall salinity load to McElmo Creek. Off-farm improvements typically consist of canal improvements such as realignments, lining, and piping. On-farm improvements typically consist of sprinkler-system and irrigation-system upgrades, including the transitional delivery system to the field. Costs associated with reducing salinity load in the Lower Colorado River rise as salinity concentration increases; therefore, understanding and managing salinity sources to the Upper Colorado River Basin potentially help reduce future water-treatment costs in the Lower Colorado River Basin (Bureau of Reclamation, 1988). The Dolores Project, located in the McElmo Creek salinity-control unit, was developed to help support the agricultural industry that farms about 62,000 acres of irrigated land in the area. The value of crops produced on the irrigated land in 1992 was estimated to be about 11 million dollars (Bureau of Reclamation, 2008). To offset the potential increase of salinity and to maintain crop productivity, salinity-control features were completed as part of the Dolores Project. These features included the reduction of canal seepage by lining, piping, rerouting canals, and combining smaller canals into a single larger canal. These features raised the efficiency of irrigation-water

applications in most areas by pressurizing water for sprinkler-irrigation systems (Bureau of Reclamation, 1988).

The USBR created a water-quality monitoring network before construction of McPhee Reservoir and implementation of salinity-control projects. Data from the network were used to estimate salinity loads in the McElmo Creek basin before implementation of the Dolores Project. The location of selected sites in the network in place before implementation of the Dolores Project, along with canals and related structures, is shown in figure 2. Samples collected at selected sites before implementation of the Dolores Project characterize salinity levels that existed when irrigation water from the Dolores River was delivered through a headgate at site 16 near the current location of McPhee Reservoir (fig. 2). The irrigation-delivery system before implementation of the Dolores Project was more prone to water shortages and short growing seasons than the new system with McPhee Reservoir. Lack of irrigation water generally has not been an issue since completion of the Dolores Project because of increased water-storage capabilities and improved water-delivery methods (Bureau of Reclamation, 1988).

Interest in understanding water and salinity budgets and the effectiveness of salinity-control efforts since the construction of McPhee Reservoir resulted in a network of water-quality monitoring sites, predominantly operated by the U.S. Geological Survey (USGS) and Colorado Division of Water Resources (CDWR). The location of selected sites in the network in place after the completion of the Dolores Project, along with canals and related structures, is shown in figure 3. Comparison of the salinity loads exiting the basin during water years 1978-1984 and water years 2000-2006 gives insight as to the effectiveness of salinity-control features that were implemented and whether additional controls are needed.

Continued interest in determining the effectiveness of salinity-control measures within the McElmo Creek basin prompted a desire for further analysis. As a result, the USGS, in cooperation with the Colorado River Salinity Control Forum (CRSCF) and the USBR, developed a study to characterize the hydrology and salinity in the McElmo Creek basin and describe the effects of salinity control efforts by comparing salinity loads before construction of the Dolores Project and after the completion of salinity-control measures associated with the Dolores Project.

Purpose and Scope

This report characterizes the hydrology and salinity in the McElmo Creek region before and after completion of the Dolores Project in southwest Colorado. Based on the available water-quality data collected by the USGS, USBR, and CDWR, this report (1) describes the hydrology, salinity concentrations, and salinity loads of the McElmo Creek basin for the water years 1978–1984 (October 1977–September 1984) and water years 2000–2006 (October 1999–September 2006); (2) compares initial estimates of increases and decreases in salinity

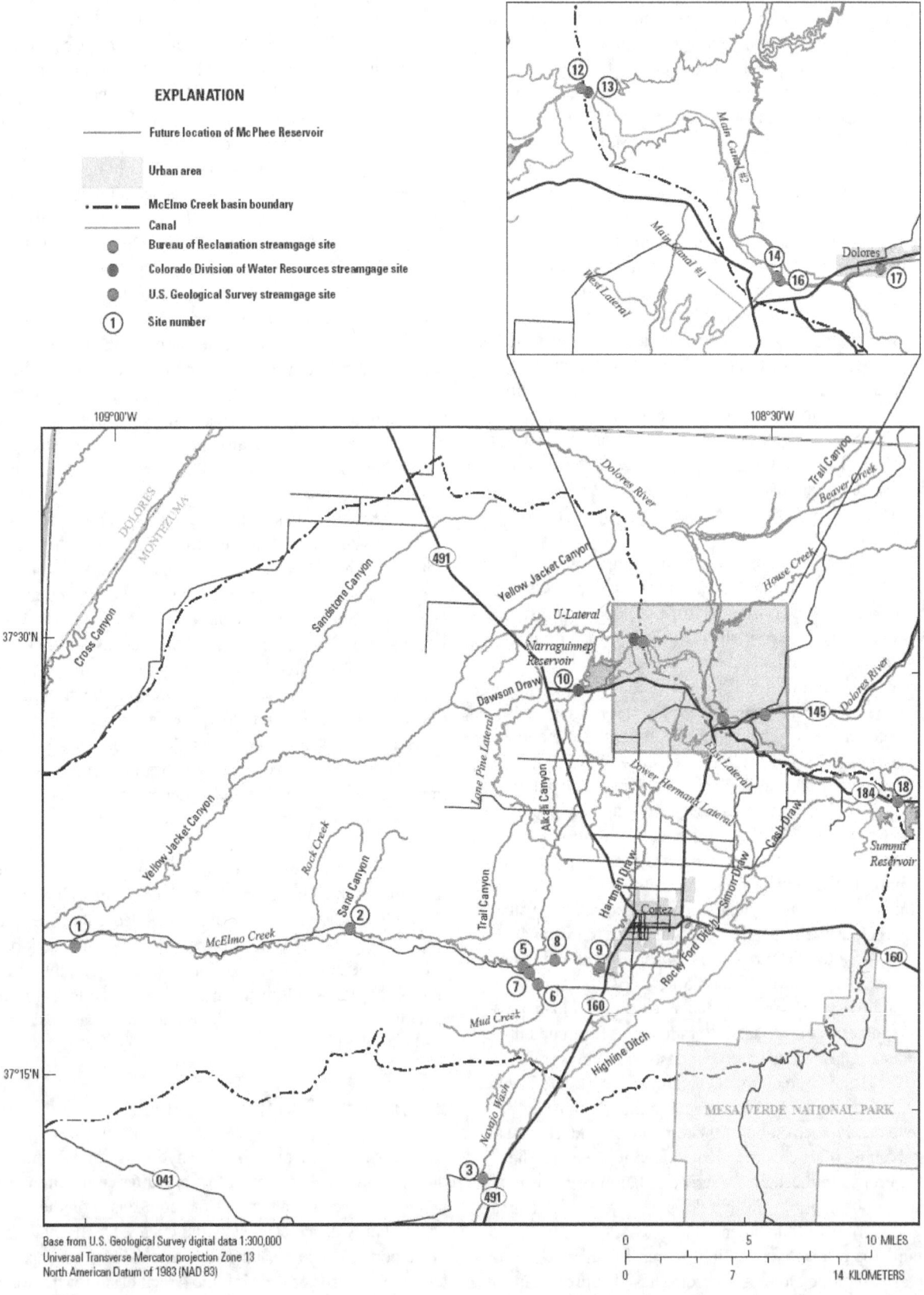

Figure 2.   Configuration of canals before construction of McPhee Reservoir, southwest Colorado.

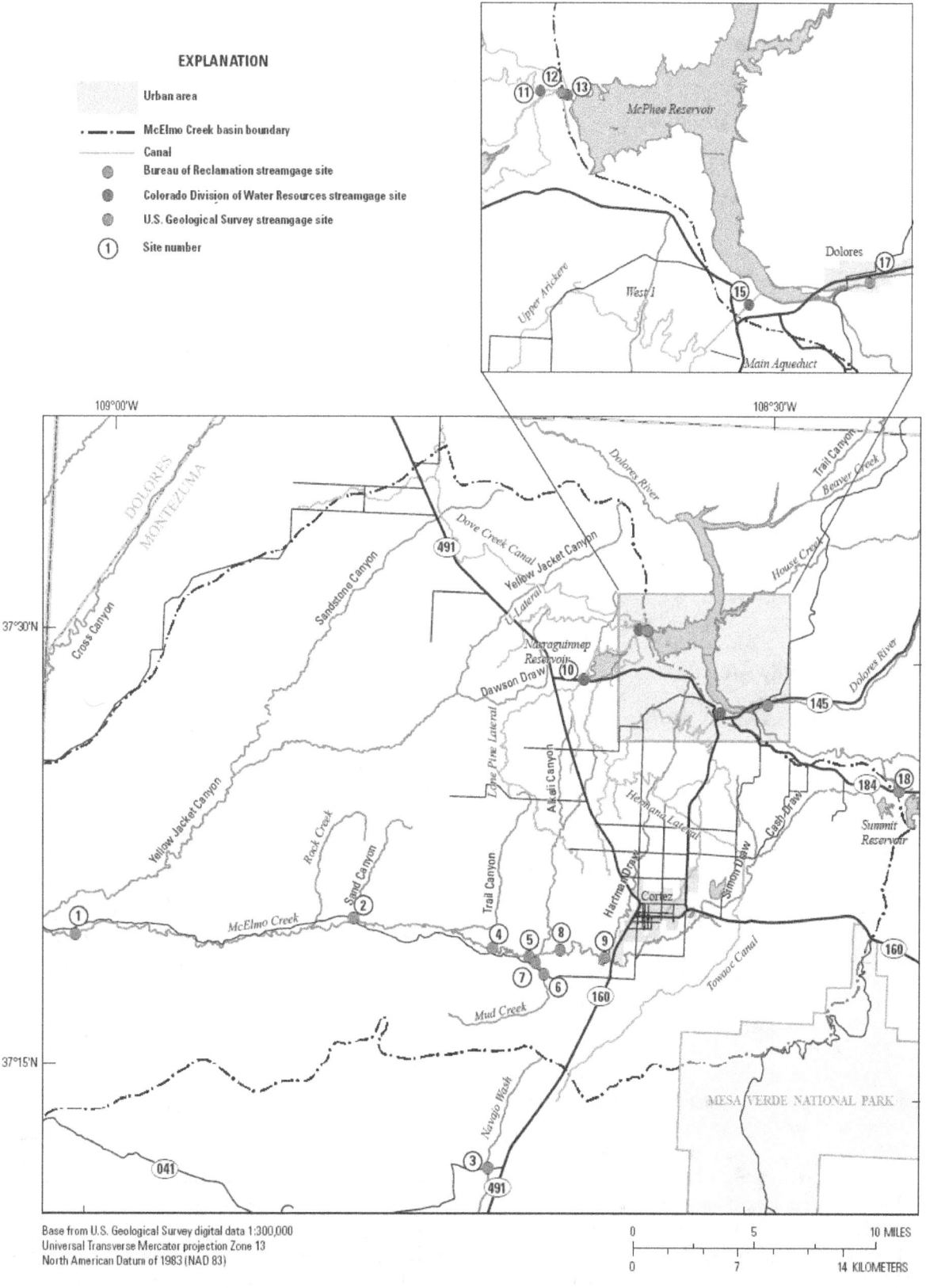

Figure 3.   Configuration of canals after construction of McPhee Reservoir, southwest Colorado.

load for the Dolores Project to measured or calculated salinity loads in the McElmo Creek basin; (3) creates a timeline that relates the Dolores Project activities to changes in streamflow and salinity concentrations and loads in McElmo Creek; and (4) characterizes natural salinity loads within McElmo Creek.

Water-quantity and water-quality data from 18 surface-water sites within and near the McElmo Creek basin were analyzed to characterize salinity concentrations and loads for water years 1978–1984 and water years 2000–2006. The date ranges represent the periods before implementation of the Dolores Project (referred to herein as the preperiod) and after the completion of the Dolores Project (referred to herein as the postperiod). Sites were selected on the basis of completeness of the water-quality record for the selected time period and location within the basin.

Flow-adjusted salinity trends over two time periods were used to characterize the magnitude and direction of salinity trend. Water years 1978–1984 were used to characterize the trend for the entire study period and include any changes in the McElmo Creek basin that resulted in changes in salinity; water years 1989–2006 were used to indicate the magnitude of the salinity trend associated with the most active salinity control efforts. A water year is defined as the 12-month period October 1 through September 30, designated by the calendar year in which it ends.

Description of Study Area

The McElmo Creek region of the Upper Colorado River Basin is located in southwest Colorado. The creek flows westward from Colorado into Utah, where it joins the San Juan River. In Colorado, McElmo Creek lies within Montezuma County between the Dolores River and the San Juan River (fig. 1). The two largest urban centers in the region are Cortez, Colorado, and Dolores, Colorado. Cortez is approximately 7 miles south of McPhee Reservoir, along the northern bank of McElmo Creek, 24 miles east from the Utah – Colorado State line. Dolores is approximately 7 miles northwest of the headwaters of McElmo Creek and east of McPhee Reservoir. The land-surface elevation at Cortez is about 6,200 feet and at Dolores is about 6,940 feet (U.S. Geological Survey Geographic Names Information System, 2008).

A substantial part of the land use in the region is irrigated agriculture (fig. 4). The agricultural lands around McElmo Creek are irrigated from a system of canals that draw water from McPhee Reservoir, Narraguinnep Reservoir, and Summit Reservoir. Residential and urban land uses are increasing as population increases in the region. The population of Cortez increased from 7,977 in 2000 to 8,531 in 2007, and the population of Dolores increased from 857 in 2000 to 905 in 2007. The population of Montezuma County increased from 23,830 in 2000 to 25,221 in 2007 (U.S. Census Bureau, 2008). The increase in population has placed increased demand on the available water supplies.

The geology of the study area is influenced by the San Juan Mountains to the east and the Monument uplift in southeast Utah. The primary geologic units at or near the surface in the study area are the Dakota Sandstone, Burro Canyon Formation, and Mancos Shale of Cretaceous age (fig. 5) (Tweto, 1979). Quaternary eolian deposits are present in the northwest part of the study area and are along some stream channels. Jurassic-age Morrison Formation and Entrada Sandstone crop out along the western reaches of McElmo Creek.

Sandstone that was deposited in or near saline environments or has been inundated by saltwater tends to have high concentrations of salts containing sodium, sulfate, chloride, magnesium, and calcium ions. As freshwater moves through porous sandstone, it mobilizes salts and transports them to streams and rivers. A similar transport of salt ions occurs in shale that was deposited in saline environments. Although not as permeable as sandstone, shale is highly porous and water that comes in contact with it or infiltrates it tends to pick up large amounts of dissolved solids (Hem, 1985).

Mancos Shale can be a substantial contributor of dissolved solids to water systems. Deposition in a marine setting increases the abundance of chloride (Cl^{2-}), sodium (Na^{1+}), magnesium (Mg^{2+}), sulfate (SO_4^{2-}), calcium (Ca^{2+}), potassium (K^{1+}), carbonic acid (HCO_3^{1-}), and carbonate (CO_3^{2-})(Garrels and Thompson, 1962). Shale deposits tend to contribute more soluble ions than associated sandstone marine deposits and typically present a higher salinity hazard (Garrels and Thompson, 1962). Mancos Shale contains appreciable amounts of gypsum, which is the predominant soluble mineral in the shale, but substantial amounts of sodium and magnesium hydrate sulfates also are present. Salt crusts (also known as effervescent salts and evaporative facies) are important contributors of salts in precipitation events. The crusts are formed from the evapoconcentration of dissolved solids after transport to the surface. Crusts develop over Mancos Shale because shale bedrock has low permeability and overland flow does not readily percolate into the soil, which allows for evaporation of water and chemical precipitation of dissolved solids.

Alluvium, which has been transported and deposited in a fluvial system, has most of its readily soluble ions removed and does not contribute dissolved constituents as much as bedrock shale deposits. Soils derived from shale typically have salt concentrations that are 10 percent higher than alluvium (Laronne, 1977).

The climate in the study area is semiarid, with some variation due to the topography and proximity of the San Juan Mountains. Based on records for 1911–2007, in Cortez, Colo., July is the hottest month, with an average maximum temperature of 88.7 degrees Fahrenheit, and January is the coldest month, with an average minimum temperature of 13.2 degrees Fahrenheit. The annual average total precipitation for Cortez during the same time period is 13.12 inches, with an average annual snowfall of 35.2 inches. In comparison, Dolores, Colo., which is slightly outside the McElmo Creek basin, received an average of 18.62 inches of precipitation annually from 1908 to 2004 and had an average annual snowfall of 65.2 inches

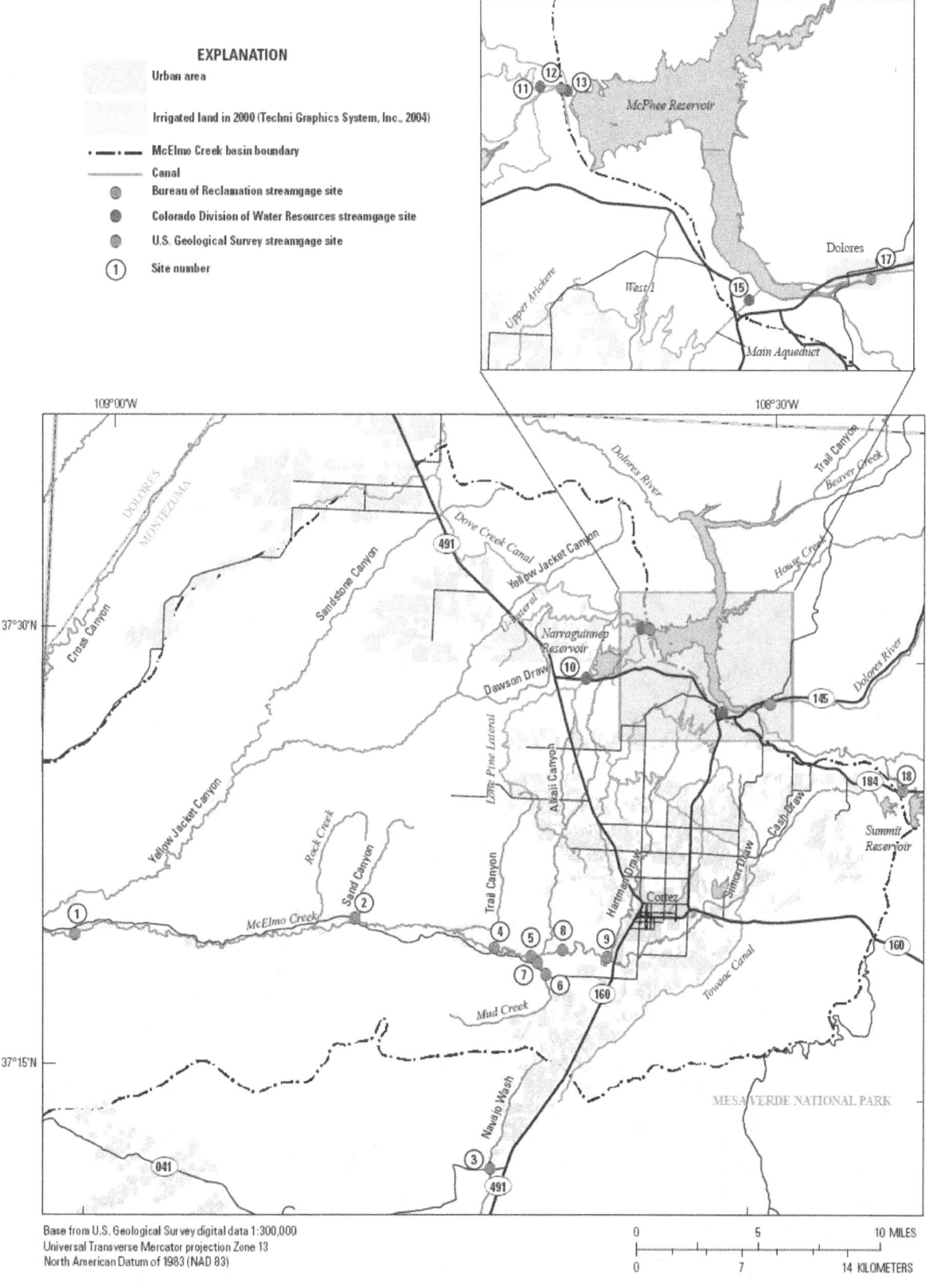

Figure 4.   Irrigated lands in the year 2000 and canal configuration after completion of McPhee Reservoir, southwest Colorado.

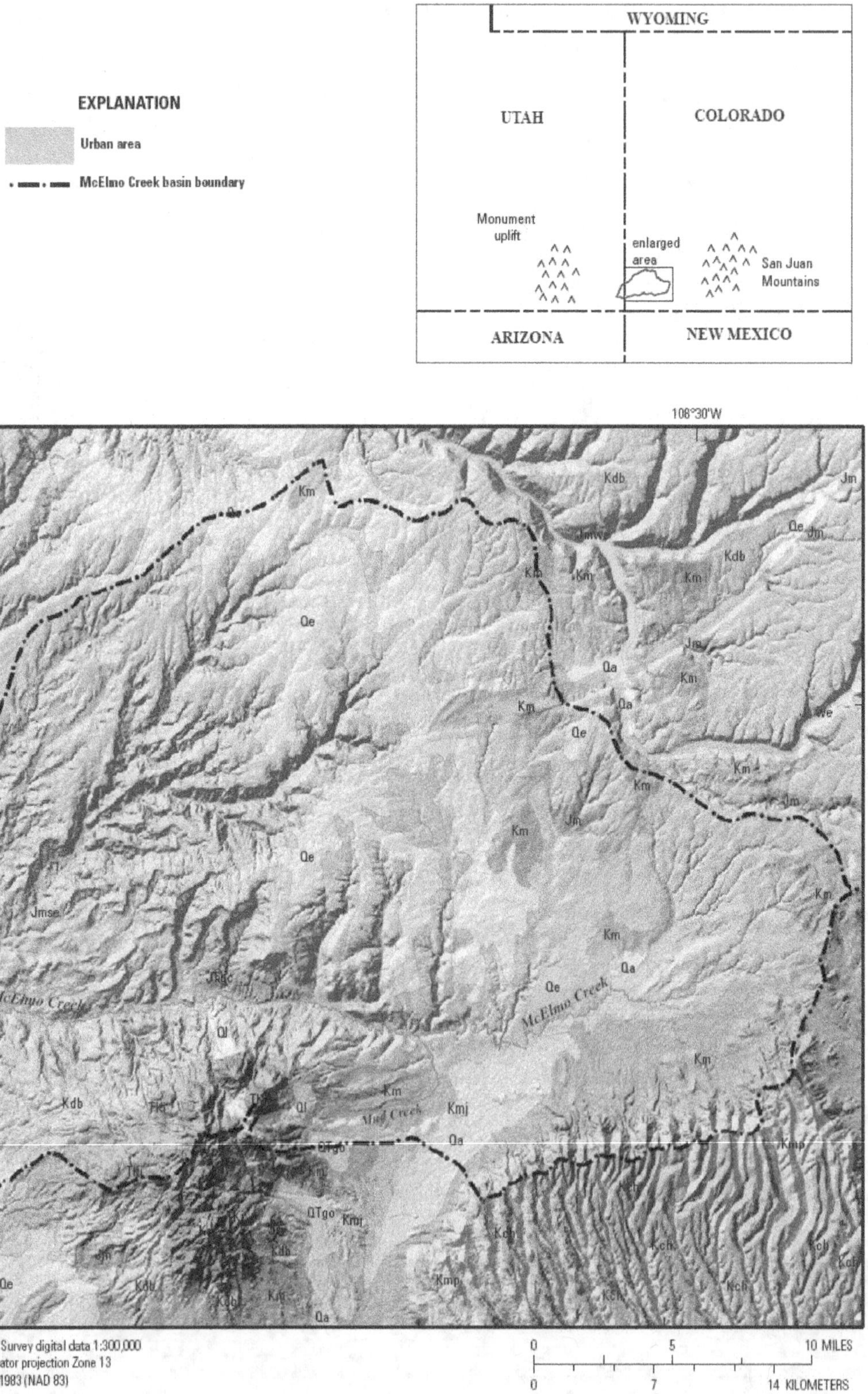

EXPLANATION

Urban area

McElmo Creek basin boundary

Figure 5.   Surficial exposures of geologic units in the McElmo Creek watershed and surrounding area.

GEOLOGY EXPLANATION

UNCONSOLIDATED SURFICIAL DEPOSITS AND ROCKS OF QUATERNARY AGE

Qa   **MODERN ALLUVIUM**—Includes Piney Creek Alluvium and younger deposits

QTgo   **OLDER GRAVELS AND ALLUVIUMS (PRE-BULL LAKE AGE)**—Includes Quaternary Verdos, Slocum, Rocky Flats, and Pliocene Nussbaum Alluviums in east, and Quaternary Florida, Bridgetimber, and Bayfield Gravels in southwest

Qe   **EOLIAN DEPOSITS**—Includes dune sand and silt and Peoria Loess

Ql   **LANDSLIDE DEPOSITS**—Locally includes talus, rock-glacier, and thick colluvial deposits

IGNEOUS ROCKS OF EARLY TERTIARY AND LATE CRETACEOUS AGE

TKi   **LARAMIDE INTRUSIVE ROCKS (AGE 40-72? M.Y.)**—Mainly intermediate to felsic compositions; some mafic

SEDIMENTARY ROCKS OF CRETACEOUS AGE

Kch   **CLIFF HOUSE SANDSTONE**

Kmp   **MENEFEE FORMATION (SANDSTONE, SHALE, AND COAL) AND POINT LOOKOUT SANDSTONE**

Km   **MANCOS SHALE**—Intertongues complexly with units of overlying Mesaverde Group or Formation; lower part consists of a calcareous Niobrara equivalent and Frontier Sandstone and Mowry Shale Members; in areas where the Frontier and Mowry Members, or these and the Dakota Sandstone are distinguished, map unit (Km) consists of shale above Frontier Member

Kmj   **Juana Lopez Member**—Calcareous sandstone; a thin but persistent unit distinguished only locally

Kdb   **DAKOTA SANDSTONE AND BURRO CANYON FORMATION**—Sandstone, shale, and conglomerate

SEDIMENTARY ROCKS OF JURASSIC AGE

Jm   **MORRISON FORMATION**—Variegated claystone, mudstone, sandstone, and local beds of limestone

Jmse   **MORRISON FORMATION, SUMMERVILLE FORMATION (SHALE AND SILTSTONE), AND ENTRADA SANDSTONE**

Jmwe   **MORRISON, WANAKAH, AND ENTRADA FORMATIONS**

SEDIMENTARY ROCKS OF JURASSIC AND TRIASSIC AGE

JTRgc   **GLEN CANYON GROUP AND CHINLE FORMATION**—In southwest, Glen Canyon Group consists of Navajo Sandstone, Kayenta Formation (red siltstone, shale, and sandstone), and Wingate Sandstone; Chinle is red siltstone

(Western Regional Climate Center, 2008). Because of the lack of precipitation in the study area, irrigation is important to sustain a productive growing season.

The Dolores Project

The Dolores Project was designed to provide water for irrigation, municipal and industrial use, power production, recreation, and wildlife enhancement to Montezuma and Dolores Counties in southwest Colorado. McPhee Reservoir was constructed as the primary storage device of the project (Bureau of Reclamation, 1988). The McElmo Creek basin was added to the Dolores Project in 1984 by Public Law 98–569, allowing for salinity-control features to be constructed in the basin to reduce potential salinity increases in McElmo Creek resulting from McPhee Reservoir (Bureau of Reclamation, 1988). Salinity control was important to the McElmo Creek basin because storage in McPhee Reservoir increased the length of the irrigation season by supplying increased late-season irrigation water. The longer irrigation season increases both the amount of irrigation water applied and the amount of time water is in contact with saline soils which, in turn, can increase the salinity load entering McElmo Creek.

Groundbreaking for the Dolores Project occurred in September 1977; however, construction of McPhee Dam did not begin until 1980. McPhee Dam was completed and McPhee Reservoir began to fill in 1984; by 1986 a full supply of irrigation water was available for use. Construction of salinity-control features in McElmo Creek basin began shortly after. By 1994, the USBR had completed realignment of the Towaoc Canal and lateral system to serve the land previously watered by the Rocky Ford Ditch and Highline Ditch. Sections of the Hermana and Lone Pine Laterals were also lined in 1994. Off-farm remediation by the USBR ended in 1994 along with the completion of the Dolores Project modifications and salinity-control features (fig. 6).

Salinity-control features included in the Dolores Project were designed to help reduce and offset the increase in salinity load from increased water usage and longer irrigation seasons. According to revised estimates by the USBR for the 1977 Dolores Project Definite Plan Report, an additional 43,150 tons of salt would enter McElmo Creek annually from project lands and canals. Realignment of the Towaoc Canal would add another 7,500 tons per year, making a total of 50,650 tons per year as a result of plan development (table 1). Salinity-control features, including the realignment of the Towaoc Canal, and project modifications were estimated to decrease the salinity load by 32,000 tons per year. Therefore, the net total project effect was estimated to increase the salinity load by 18,650 tons per year. These estimates do not include any on-farm irrigation controls for decreasing salinity loading (Bureau of Reclamation, 1988).

Methods of Analysis

Site Selection

Sites in the McElmo Creek study area were selected by their location relative to McElmo Creek and the amount of available data associated with each site. Sites that lacked a continuous data record or had missing values that could not be estimated using regression analysis for either the pre-period or the postperiod were not used in the data analysis. The USBR, USGS, and CDWR operated sites in and near the McElmo Creek basin that were used in the analysis (table 2; fig. 1). Data for the USBR sites were used mostly for analysis of preperiod streamflow and water quality, whereas the USGS data were used mostly for analysis of postperiod streamflow and water quality. The CDWR data were used for determination of canal flow and diversion amounts for both preperiod and postperiod.

From July 1972 to February 1984, streamflow and water-quality data were collected by the USBR before and during the implementation of the salinity-control features of the Dolores Project. Data for this period, including field measurements and laboratory analyses, were extracted by physical examination of 12 volumes of historical hardcopy records (on file at Bureau of Reclamation, Durango office, Durango, Colo.). The extracted data were entered into spreadsheet format for analysis and preservation.

Quality assurance for site name and location was established by importing the data into a Geographic Information Systems (GIS) database using the attribute records of quarter-section, township, range, and local-vicinity description. Sites with inconsistent or changed names were assigned a single unique name and an explanatory remark was entered in the database. Any modifications of names and locations made for this study were verified by USBR personnel associated with the Dolores Project sampling activity. Sites duplicating an existing USGS site were assigned a USGS name, a station number, and a remark code in the database. Records without a verified location and date were removed from the active dataset.

The records in the active dataset were required to meet minimum criteria for salinity-load calculations. Each record had to contain a daily streamflow value and either a daily TDS value or a daily specific-conductance (SC) value. Specific conductance is a measure of the ability of water to conduct an electrical current and can be used to estimate TDS (Mills and others, 1993).

USGS water-quality sampling sites within the McElmo Creek basin and adjacent drainages were identified. The water-quality data were retrieved from the USGS National Water Information System (NWIS) database for selected sites at *http://nwis.waterdata.usgs.gov/nwis*. Water-quality data consisted of daily mean streamflow and daily mean SC values. Water-quality data were analyzed using standard USGS

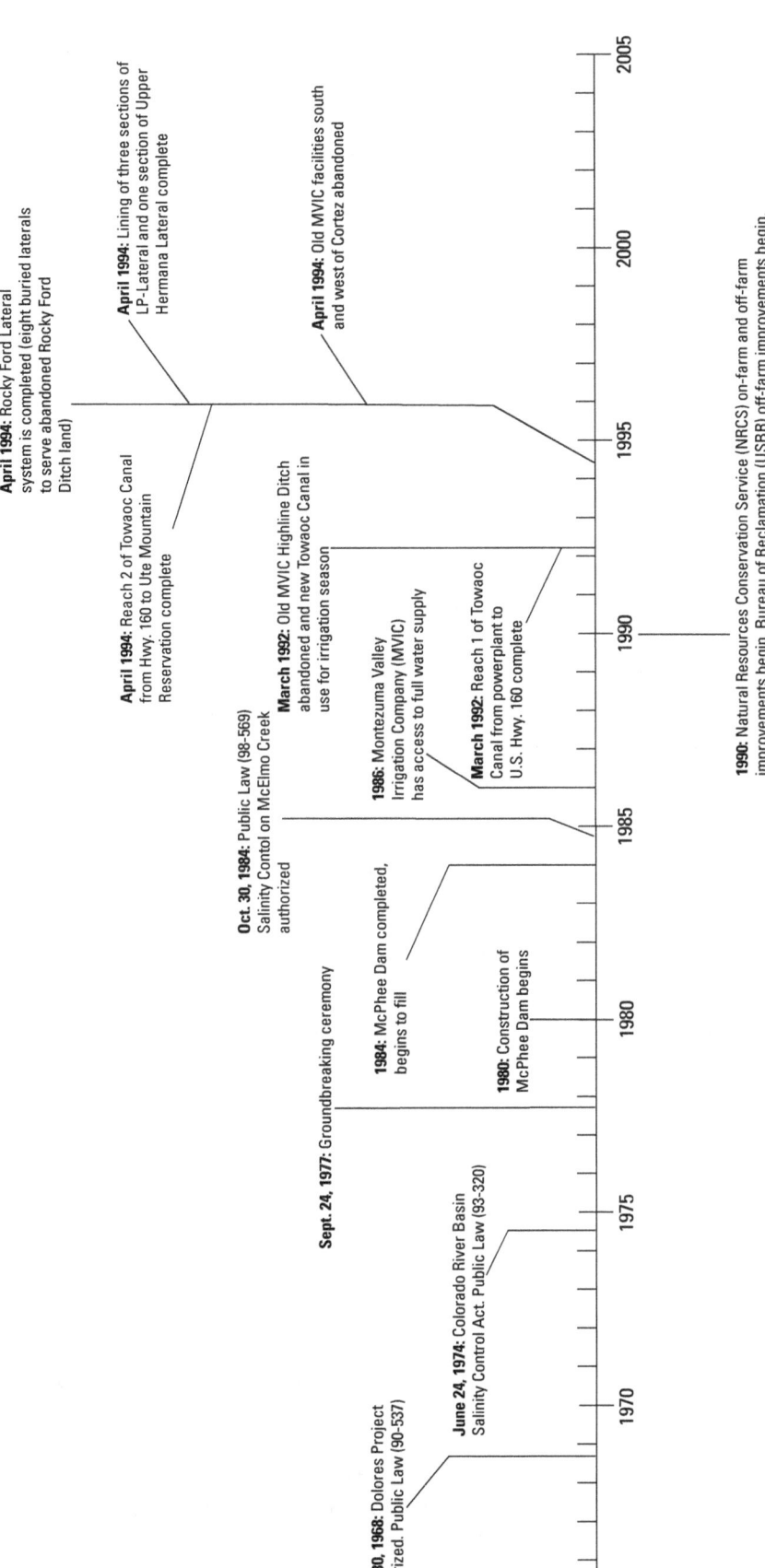

Figure 6.   Timeline of events related to the completion of the Dolores Project from 1965 through 2004.

Table 1. Initial and updated estimates of salinity loading as a result of the Dolores Project, southwest Colorado.

[Estimates from Dolores Project Report (Bureau of Reclamation, 1988); DPR, Dolores Project Report; USBR, Bureau of Reclamation]

DPR elements	Initial salinity loading in 1977 DPR plan, in tons per year	Updated salinity loading for the 1977 DPR plan, in tons per year	Change in salinity loading resulting from project modifications, in tons per year	USBR estimated salinity loading for the plan of development, in tons per year
Dolores Project Area—Projected lands and canals	10,080[1]	43,150[2]	0	43,150
Towaoc Canal—West alignment	0	7,500	−7,500	0
Salinity control features	0	0	−24,500	−24,000
Total project effect	10,080	50,650	−32,000	18,650

[1]Original DPR plan did not account for canal seepage.

[2]Canal seepage accounted for in salinity load calculation.

Table 2. Water-quality sites used in the analysis of salinity load in the McElmo Creek basin, southwest Colorado.

[Sampling agency: USGS, U.S. Geological Survey; USBR, Bureau of Reclamation; CDWR, Colorado Division of Water Resources; --, no data available]

Site number (fig. 1)	Sampling site identifier	Sampling site name	Latitude	Longitude	Sampling agency	Period of sampling activity, in water years
1	09372000	McElmo Creek near Colorado-Utah State line	37°19'22"	109°00'54"	USGS USBR	1977–2006 1972–1989
2	09371700	McElmo Creek below Cortez, CO	37°19'22"	108°40'21"	USGS USBR	1977–2006 1972–1989
3	09371002	Navajo Wash near Towaoc, CO	37°12'03"	108°41'50"	USGS USBR	1986–1994 1982–1983
4	09371520	McElmo Creek above Trail Canyon near Cortez, CO	37°19'36"	108°42'00"	USGS USBR	1990–2006 --
5	09371500	McElmo Creek near Cortez, CO	37°19' 22"	108°40'21"	USGS USBR	1982–1993 1978–1982
6	09371492	Mud Creek at State Hwy 32 near Cortez, CO	37°18'46"	108°39'38"	USGS USBR	1982–2006 1973–1978
7	09371495	Mud Creek near Cortez, CO	37°19'10"	108°40'03"	USGS USBR	1978–1981 1972–1983
8	09371420	McElmo Creek above Alkali Canyon near Cortez, CO	37°19'38"	108°38'55"	USGS USBR	1977–1986 1972–1982
9	09371400	Hartman Draw at Cortez, CO	37°19'26"	108°36'52"	USGS USBR	1978–1990 1978–1982, 2007
10	LPHB	Lone Pine Canal at Hwy Bridge	37°28'57"	108°38'20"	CDWR	1974–2006
11	UCANALCO	U-Lateral Canal below Great Cut	37°30'45"	108°35'52"	CDWR	1977–2006
12	--	Lone Pine Lateral	37°30'42"	108°35'29"	USBR	1978, 1986–2006
13	--	U-Lateral Montezuma Valley Irrigation Company	37°30'43"	108°37'27"	CDWR	1981–2006
14	--	Main Canal #2	37°28'10"	108°31'47"	USBR	1977–1984
15	DOLTUNCO	Dolores Tunnel Outlet near Dolores, CO	37°28'00"	108°32'01"	CDWR	1985–2006
16	B100	Main Canal #1	37°28'08"	108°31'43"	USBR	1977–1985
17	09166500	Dolores River at Dolores, CO	37°38'21"	108°29'49"	USGS USBR	1977–2006
18	--	Summit Reservoir Outlet at Hwy	37°25'32"	108°23'43"	USBR	1979–1981

techniques and procedures (U.S. Geological Survey, variously dated). Sites relevant to the study area were categorized by date of available data, location, and quality of data. Data analysis included 10 USGS sites containing 1,728 discrete water-quality samples intermittently collected from water year 1978 to 2006.

Data collected by the CDWR were obtained through the CDWR online archived-data retrieval program (*http://www.dwr.state.co.us/SurfaceWater/data/rtarchive.aspx,* accessed January 10, 2008). Daily mean streamflow records of locally operated canals were obtained through the Colorado Decision Support System (CDSS) online Flood DSS Map Viewer (*http://165.127.23.41/website/FloodIMS/viewer.htm,* accessed January 10, 2008) and CDSS Stream Flow Data Selector (*http://cdss.state.co.us/Streamflow/StreamFlow.aspx,* accessed January 10, 2008). Questions regarding station names, locations, and streamflow discrepancies due to transbasin water diversions were directed to the CDWR, Water Division 7, San Juan/Dolores River basins branch-office water commissioner in Durango, Colo. Data analysis included continuous daily mean values for water years 1978 to 2006 for four CDWR sites. A record of collected samples used in this report can be obtained from the USGS Colorado Water-Quality Data Repository online at *http://rmgsc.cr.usgs.gov/cwqdr/Southwest/index.shtml.*

Data Analysis

Multivariate Regression Models

Multivariate regression models were developed for sites along McElmo Creek to calculate daily streamflow, SC, and TDS concentration, loads, and trends within the dataset. Regression analysis is useful to determine relations between multiple variables. Estimations of values for a response (y) variable can be calculated based on the values of a second explanatory (x) variable (Helsel and Hirsch, 2002). Response variables are the output value of the equation and are dependent of the explanatory variable, which is the input variable and acts independent of the response variable. Explanatory variables considered for the regressions included streamflow, SC, and a seasonal or periodic variable. A continuous dataset allowed for the use of daily or monthly regression outputs to define load. Daily values help to more accurately predict load. The regressions were developed using periodic data collected in the field. Continuous SC data were not always available for estimating TDS values. Therefore, gaps in the SC record were predicted from SC data available at an adjacent site by using a maintenance of variance extension, type 1 (Hirsch, 1982).

In order for a linear regression to be developed, assumptions had to be made about the representative sample population of the dataset for a given site. To accurately predict a response variable, the relation between response variable and explanatory variable needs to be linear and residuals normally distributed with similar variance over a range of predicted

values. Typical plots of streamflow relative to TDS have a curvilinear shape as a result of a variable TDS-concentration-to-streamflow ratio at different times of the year. To normalize a regression model, the data of x, or y, or both x and y need to be transformed to eliminate the curvature and heteroscedacity in the data (Helsel and Hirsch, 2002). Transformation of the McElmo Creek streamflow data was required to remove curvature and heteroscedacity. A natural-log transformation was chosen to create an acceptable linearization of the data. The data used to fit the model also need to represent the data of interest (Helsel and Hirsch, 2002). Residual plots (where the residual is the estimated value minus the correlating observed value) are necessary to determine whether a normal distribution is present. A normal distribution is important when testing the hypothesis for confidence.

The multivariate regression models also included a seasonal term. The seasonal term was applied to adjust (or account) for the relation between streamflow and the irrigation season of McElmo Creek region. The seasonal variable is based on a Julian date and herein is referred to as a dummy variable. The dummy variable is assigned a value of 0 for the irrigation season and a value of 1 for the nonirrigation season. The irrigation season in the McElmo Creek region typically is from April through October, and the nonirrigation season is from November through March.

Multivariate regression models were derived using ordinary least-squares (OLS) regression with S-PLUS 7.0 software (Insightful Corp., 2005a). The statistical applicability of each model was determined using regression diagnostics such as the coefficient of determination (R^2), standard error of estimate, and p-values, which indicate the probability the slope is zero, for individual variables. Models with R^2 values greater than 0.70 and a homoscedastic distribution of residuals were considered acceptable. Models with R^2 values less than 0.70 were rejected and other variable combinations were then tested. The larger the p-value, the less likely the variables are related. Models with p-values greater than 0.05 were rejected because such values indicated an unacceptable correlation between variables. Standard error of estimate is an estimate of the standard deviation of the residuals about the regression. Smaller values of the standard error of estimate mean the representation of the prediction is more accurate (Driver and Tasker, 1990). Plots of residuals also were used to help identify normality. Residual plots for appropriate models show little to no curvature or change in shape. Residual plots relative to time also were created to determine if a correlation exists. The presence of a correlation indicates that a sampling bias or a trend exists (Helsel and Hirsch, 2002). All of these diagnostics were used in evaluating regression models and determining trends in the dataset.

Salinity-Load Calculations

Salinity load is the amount of salt that is transported by a water body; salinity load typically is reported here in units of tons per unit of time. Salinity loads were determined as the product of streamflow and the concentration of TDS. Two types of TDS data were used in this report, sum of constituents (SOC) and residue on evaporation (ROE). SOC is the sum of the total soluble anion and cation concentrations. ROE is the residue remaining after a given volume of water is evaporated for a given amount of time at a given temperature. ROE has potential for error due to organic matter that might not be completely volatilized, or from the presence of hydrophilic residues such as gypsum-laden sulfates (Hem, 1985). When applicable, SOC was used preferentially over ROE for regression analysis.

When daily TDS data were available, daily salinity load was calculated using the following equation:

$$L_s = TDS\,(Q)\,0.0027 \tag{1}$$

where

L_S	is the daily salinity load, in tons,
TDS	is the measured daily TDS concentration, in milligrams per liter,
Q	is the daily mean streamflow, in cubic feet per second, and
0.0027	is the unit constant to obtain tons per day from milligrams per liter and cubic feet per second.

When TDS data were not available to use in equation 1, a TDS value was estimated using a regression model based on SC.

A TDS value was calculated as a function of SC by using the following equation:

$$TDS_e = \beta_0 + \beta_1(SC) \tag{2}$$

where

TDS_e	is the estimated TDS concentration in milligrams per liter,
SC	is the daily mean SC in microsiemens per centimeter at 25° Celsius, and
β_n	are regression coefficients.

The estimated TDS concentration (TDS_e) was then substituted into equation 1 for daily salinity-load calculations. The form of equation 2 used at selected sites in the McElmo Creek basin is summarized in table 3.

Missing SC values were estimated by using an upstream site with available SC data. The record extension technique, Maintenance of Variance Extension, Type 1 (MOVE.1) was used. MOVE.1 is an alternative to the standard regression approach and maintains the sample mean and variance in the dataset. SC data for McElmo Creek above Trail Canyon near Cortez (site 4), McElmo Creek near Cortez (site 5), and Hartman Draw at Cortez (site 9) were used to determine missing SC values for McElmo Creek near the Colorado–Utah State line (site 1). These were chosen to predict SC at site 1 because they are the closest upstream sites on the main stem of McElmo Creek. The site used to predict the SC at site 1 was determined by SC data availability during the period of missing SC values from site 1. When multiple sites had

overlapping SC data for a needed time period, the closest upstream site was used. SC values for missing dates were estimated by using the following equation:

$$SC_e = \bar{y} + \frac{Sy}{Sx}(x_i - \bar{x}) \tag{3}$$

where

SC_e	is the estimated SC value at site 1, in microsiemens per centimeter at 25° Celsius,
$\bar{y}$	is the sample mean of observed SC values at site 1,
$\bar{x}$	is the sample mean of observed values at a selected adjacent site,
Sy	is the standard deviation of observed values at site 1,
Sx	is the standard deviation of observed values at a selected adjacent site, and
x_i	is the observed SC value of a selected adjacent site.

The estimated SC value was then used in equation 2 to estimate the TDS concentration.

A 3-year moving-average regression equation was also used to estimate missing daily SC values. When SC data from an adjacent site were not available for use in equation 3, equation 4 was used to fill in missing daily values. The 3-year moving-average regression uses data for a 3-year period to determine the SC value for a given day in the middle year in the selected period. The period then moves 1 year forward and the calculation is repeated for the next year to be calculated (Kircher and others, 1984). Estimations of SC data using a 3-year moving-average regression were calculated using the equation:

$$\ln SC_e = \beta_0 + \beta_1 \ln Q + \beta_2 D \tag{4}$$

where

$\ln SC_e$	is the natural logarithm of specific conductance, in microsiemens per centimeter,
β_n	are regression coefficients,
$\ln Q$	is the natural logarithm of daily mean streamflow at McElmo Creek near the Colorado–Utah State line, in cubic feet per second, and
D	is a dummy variable where 1 was used for the nonirrigation season and 0 for the irrigation season.

The resulting SC value was then used in equation 2 to estimate the TDS concentration. By using a predicted value of SC to predict TDS, errors are introduced. Karlinger and Troutman (1985) indicate that biases in the regression line and error variance are a function of lacking a correlation between independent and dependent variables, and errors associated with a cascade-regression prediction can be large.

Estimates of daily salinity loads from Mud Creek, which drains into McElmo Creek, were calculated using data from two sites, Mud Creek near Cortez (site 7) and Mud Creek at State Hwy 32 (site 6). These data were used in equation 1 to

Table 3. Summary of equations used to estimate TDS at selected sites in the McElmo Creek region, southwest Colorado.

[TDS, total dissolved solids; ln, natural logarithm; SC, specific conductance; R2, coefficient of determination]

Site number (fig. 1)	Period of record used	Equation	Intercept	Coefficient	R2
1	1978–1983	TDS = 0.8722(SC) – 61.363	–61.363	0.8722	0.832
	1984–1999	TDS = 0.9771(SC) – 354.71	–354.71	0.9771	0.950
	2000–2006	TDS = 0.9687(SC) – 371.81	–371.81	0.9687	0.993
3	1987–1994	TDS = 0.9897(SC) – 465.19	–465.19	0.9897	0.991
6	1982–1986	lnTDS = 1.1436(ln SC) – 1.3519	–1.3519	1.1436	0.991
	1994–2006	lnTDS = 1.1506 (ln SC) – 1.4058	–1.4058	1.1506	0.997
7	1979–1981	TDS = 1.2127(SC) – 869.319	–869.319	1.2127	0.987
15	1978–2006	TDS = 0.5999(SC) – 0.3666	–0.3666	0.5999	0.932

estimate salinity load. Data records for site 6 exist for water years 1973–1978 and water years 1982–2006. Data records for site 7 are available for water years 1972–1983. Because neither site had a complete preperiod record, data for site 7 were used for water years 1978–1981 and data for site 6 were used for water years 1982–1984. For the postperiod, data for site 6 were used exclusively because no data had been collected at site 7 since 1983. Data from the two sites were compiled and used to calculate the daily salinity loads for Mud Creek. These salinity-load estimates are assumed to represent the entire Mud Creek basin.

Data for site 7 for water years 1979–1983 were used in equation 2 to calculate missing TDS data for the salinity-load estimates (table 3). If SC data were missing, equation 3 was used. The resulting TDS values were then entered into equation 1 to estimate salinity load. Few streamflow and SC data were available for water years 1982–1983; therefore, data from site 7 were only used for water years 1979–1981.

Data from site 6 were used to calculate the daily salinity load for water years 1982–2006 (table 3). Daily salinity load was determined using equation 1. In the absence of TDS data, equation 2 was used to estimate TDS. When SC data were not available, the data were calculated using equation 3 and then entered into equation 2. The resulting TDS values were then entered into equation 1 to estimate salinity load.

The Navajo Wash basin was included in the McElmo Creek salinity-load estimations because it collects irrigation return water from irrigated lands within the Dolores Project area and receives the water that is left in Towaoc Canal at its terminus. The decommissioned Rocky Ford Ditch, along with the Highline Ditch and the Towaoc Canal, supplied water to irrigated lands that had return flow into Navajo Wash. Data for USGS streamgaging station 09371002 Navajo Wash near Towaoc, CO (site 3) allow for estimation of salinity loads discharging from the McElmo Creek basin through Navajo Wash. Data associated with site 3 are sparse and mostly incomplete. Therefore, salinity-load data during the preperiod from water year 1982 to 1984 were estimated from available

salinity data available from the USBR (on file at Bureau of Reclamation, Durango, Colo.). Data for the postperiod were sporadic and incomplete, making it very difficult to calculate a salinity load. Because of the geographic and geologic similarities of Navajo Wash basin to the Mud Creek basin, the salinity load at site 3 was assumed to be similar to that at site 6 for both periods. Therefore, the salinity load discharging at site 3 during the preperiod was multiplied by the postperiod percent-change factor for site 6 as a means to estimate the salinity load discharging at site 3 for the postperiod. The salinity load for site 3 for the preperiod was calculated using equations 1–4 as shown herein.

Trend Analysis

The S-Plus load-computing program Load Estimator (S-LOADEST) was used to assist in the evaluation of time trends in the dataset. S-LOADEST calculates loads based on a model developed by the user. The load outputs and residuals can then be evaluated for trends. Plots of the residuals are checked for homoscedacity, linearity, and constant variance to identify a model of best fit.

Plots of the partial residuals can be used to assess trends within a dataset. Partial residuals are the difference between an observed value of y and a predicted value of y from a regression equation where an explanatory variable of interest (such as time) is left out of the model, while all other explanatory variables are present. The partial residual plot describes the relation between y and the explanatory variable left out of the model after all effects of the other explanatory variables have been removed (Helsel and Hirsch, 2002).

A LOcally WEighted Scatterplot Smoothing (LOWESS) curve can also be used to evaluate whether a trend exists in the partial residual data set. The LOWESS curve can be useful in indicating where changes in the trend occur that are not visible just from analyzing data points in the partial residual plot. LOWESS is an approach to smoothing using a noise-reduction algorithm (Insightful Corp., 2005b). LOWESS describes the relation between x and y variables, and the partial residuals are not assumed to be linear or normalized. LOWESS smoothing is a robust description of the pattern formed by the data (Helsel and Hirsch, 2002). When homoscedacity, linearity, and constant variance are met, linear trends in the dataset are assessed. S-LOADEST can then be used to calculate the load for a beginning year of choice and an ending year of choice; the difference in load of the selected years can be used to estimate any upward or downward trend that might exist for the calculated load based on time (TIBCO, 2008).

Data for sites 1, 6, and 17 were analyzed for trends during the study period from water years 1978 to 2006. Regression models were calibrated in the statistical software S-LOADEST based on the FORTRAN version developed by Runkel and others (2004). The equation for each site was calibrated using data for all available discrete, intermittent water-quality samples within the study-period timeframe. Initially a seven-parameter model was used in this report, incorporating flow dependence, time trends, and seasonality. Accounting for differences in seasonality can also be accomplished using an irrigation season "dummy variable" and a pair of trigonometric variables that define an annual cycle. The following seven-parameter model was used:

$$\ln\hat{L} = \beta_0 + \beta_1(\ln Q - \ln Q^*) + \beta_2(\ln Q - \ln Q^*)^2 + \beta_3(t - t^*) \quad (5)$$
$$+ \beta_4(t - t^*)^2 + \beta_5\sin(K2\pi T) + \beta_6\cos(K2\pi T) + \beta_7 D$$

where

$\ln\hat{L}$ is the natural logarithm of predicted salinity load, in tons per day;

β_0 is the regression equation intercept;

β_n is the coefficient for the regression variable n;

$\ln Q$ is the natural logarithm of daily mean streamflow, in cubic feet per second;

$\ln Q^*$ is the natural logarithm of streamflow, centered for the calibration dataset, in cubic feet per second;

t is time, in decimal years;

t^* is the time, centered for the calibration dataset, in decimal years;

$\sin(K2\pi T)$ and $\cos(K2\pi T)$ are seasonality terms, where K is an integer and T is the decimal portion of the year starting January 1; and

D is a seasonality "dummy" variable for irrigation and nonirrigation seasons.

Additional information can be found in Cohn (2005).

Explanatory variables were orthogonalized to "center" the data and remove any multicolinearity of the explanatory variables, which can create load estimation errors (Runkel and others, 2004). These data were "centered" using the following equations described by Cohn and others (1992):

$$\ln Q^* = \ln\overline{Q} + \frac{\sum_{i=1}^{N}(\ln Q_i - \ln\overline{Q})^3}{2\sum_{i=1}^{N}(\ln Q_i - \ln\overline{Q})^2} \quad \text{and} \quad \ln\overline{Q} = \frac{\sum_{i=1}^{N}\ln Q_i}{N} \quad (6)$$

where

$\ln Q^*$ is the natural logarithm of streamflow, centered for the calibration dataset, in cubic feet per second;

$\ln\overline{Q}$ is the mean of the natural logarithm of streamflow in the dataset, in cubic feet per second;

$\ln Q_i$ is the natural logarithm of daily mean streamflow for day i, in cubic feet per second; and

N is the number of daily values in the dataset.

$$t^* = \overline{t} + \frac{\sum_{i=1}^{N}(t_i - \overline{t})^3}{2\sum_{i=1}^{N}(t_i - \overline{t})^2} \quad \text{and} \quad \overline{t} = \frac{\sum_{i=1}^{N}t_i}{N} \quad (7)$$

where

t^* is the time, centered for the calibration dataset, in decimal years;

$\overline{t}$ is the mean of the time in the dataset, in decimal years;

t_i is time for day i, in decimal years; and

N is the number of daily values in the dataset.

If logarithmic transformations are used for the response variable, a bias is produced when the logarithms of the estimated values are retransformed to original units. An underestimation of the mean response typically results, and the majority of the bias can be eliminated by multiplying the estimated response by a bias-correction factor (Duan, 1983). This bias correction was done by the S-LOADEST software, and no manual calculation was necessary. For details on transformation and bias-correction factors see Runkel and others (2004), Cohn and others (1989), and Likes (1980).

The S-LOADEST program estimates regression coefficients using an Adjusted Maximum Likelihood Estimation (AMLE) method (Cohn, 1989). This method gives the same results as standard MLE method if there are no censored values in the dataset. S-LOADEST calculates the loads based on the calibrated regression model for each site. S-LOADEST also calculates a salinity concentration from the estimated load by dividing the load by the flow value and conversion factor. Salinity loads and concentrations were estimated for the entire study period (water years 1978–2006) and for a period of time designated as having high levels of salinity-control activity and expected visible trends (water years 1989–2006). A summary of the best-fit model, which was derived from the seven-parameter model, used for sites 1, 6, and 17 is given in table 4. Statistical diagnostics are summarized in table 5. An important note is that centered SC was a significant explanatory variable in the regression equations but was not used in the S-LOADEST equations because mean daily values for SC were not available for site 1 and site 17, and SC was not a significant variable for site 6.

Table 4. Summary of equation forms used to estimate salinity load at the sampling sites.

[$\hat{L}$, salinity load, in tons per day; B_0, coefficient that is the y-axis intercept in the regression model; B_n, estimated coefficients of the explanatory variable; Q, daily mean streamflow, in cubic feet per second; Q*, streamflow centered for the calibration dataset, in cubic feet per second; t, time, in decimal years; t*, time centered for the calibration dataset, in decimal years; T, seasonality term representing the decimal portion of the year; K, an integer]

Site number (fig. 1)	Response variable		Explanatory variable		Equation form
	Variable	Transformation	Variable	Transformation	
1	$\hat{L}$	Natural log	Q,Q* t, t*,T	Natural log None	$\ln L = B_0 + B_1(\ln Q - \ln Q^*) + B_2(t - t^*) + B_3\sin(2\pi T) + B_4\cos(2\pi T)$
6	$\hat{L}$	Natural log	Q,Q* t, t*,T	None	$\ln L = B_0 + B_1(\ln Q - \ln Q^*) + B_2(t - t^*) + B_3\sin(2\pi T) + B_4\cos(2\pi T) + B_5\sin(K2\pi T) + B_6(K2\pi T)$
17	$\hat{L}$	Natural log	Q,Q* t, t*,T	Natural log None	$\ln L = B_0 + B_1(\ln Q - \ln Q^*) + B_2(t - t^*) + B_3\sin(2\pi T) + B_4\cos(2\pi T) + B_5\sin(K2\pi T) + B_6(K2\pi T)$

Table 5. Summary of regression model coefficients and diagnostics for three sampling sites.

[Q, daily mean streamflow, in cubic feet per second; Q*, streamflow centered for the calibration dataset, in cubic feet per second; T, seasonality term representing the decimal portion of the year; K, an integer; t, time, in decimal years; t*, time centered for the calibration dataset, in decimal years; ERV, estimated residual variance; SCR, serial correlation of the residuals; R2, coefficient of determination; --, no data]

Site number	Y-axis intercept	Streamflow		Seasonality variables Fourier series				Dummy variable	Decimal time		Statistical diagnostics		
				2πT		K2πT							
		lnQ	lnQ*	Sin	Cos	Sin	Cos		t	t*	ERV	SCR	R2
1	5.0303	0.8340	26.06	0.1240	0.2655	--	--	--	-0.0141	1991.86	0.0156	0.233	97.55
6	3.6446	0.7332	4.598	0.0781	0.3098	-0.1304	-0.0277	--	-0.0457	1991.21	0.0264	0.1329	92.79
17	5.0259	0.7546	340.5	0.0455	0.1289	0.0186	-0.04023	--	-0.0047	1990.57	0.0179	0.0609	98.51

Outliers also were evaluated and compared to the rest of the dataset. Outliers that were not consistent with the normal flow regime, such as high streamflows resulting from large rainstorms that created abnormal data points, were removed from the dataset in order to prevent a false trend. One outlier was removed from the site 6 dataset and one removed from the site 17 dataset because they appeared to be the result of monsoonal-type rainstorms that did not fit the rest of the dataset.

Characterization of Hydrology and Salinity in McElmo Creek

The streamflow regime of McElmo Creek is based largely on seasonal moisture patterns, along with regulated releases from Summit Reservoir and McPhee Reservoir. Typical with other alpine headwater streams, seasonal streamflow is dependent on snow moisture content and the timing and intensity of rainfall and snowmelt. Water quality in McElmo Creek is affected by seasonal changes in streamflow pattern. TDS

concentration changes frequently with changing flow conditions, moisture patterns, and regulated releases from McPhee Reservoir and Summit Reservoir. Dilution occurs when increased water is supplied to the system. Dilution typically occurs during spring runoff and intense storms. However, increasing the amount of water to the system also can flush salts into the stream and can create large increases in TDS from the dissolution of near-surface salt deposits.

Hydrology

Streamflow patterns vary throughout the McElmo Creek region. Streamflow data are summarized in table 6. Streamflow rate in McElmo Creek fluctuates as water moves downstream. Irrigation withdrawals decrease flow in the stream, whereas water gained from tributaries increases flow. Mean daily streamflow for the McElmo Creek region for the study period ranged from 6.31 ft³/s at site 7 to 57.3 ft³/s at site 5 (fig. 7, table 6). Daily streamflow values for study sites in the

Table 6. Summary of daily streamflow data for selected steamgaging stations in or near the McElmo Creek basin, southwest Colorado.

[Site name, U.S. Geological Survey (USGS) station name; ft³/s, cubic feet per second; Max, maximum; Min, minimum; # Obs, number of observations]

Site name	Site number (fig.1)	USGS site identifier	Period of record	Daily streamflow, ft³/s				
				Max	Min	Mean	Median	# Obs
Dolores River at Dolores, CO	17	09166500	1900/01/01–1903/10/01, 1910/10/01–1912/19/30, 1921/10/01–2005/12/28	6,950	11.00	434	123	32,900
Hartman Draw at Cortez, CO	9	09371400	1978/04/01–1986/09/30	104	0.28	13.6	11.0	3,110
McElmo Creek above Alkali Canyon, near Cortez, CO	8	09371420	1972/10/01–1986/09/30	302	1.50	27.4	20.0	5,110
McElmo Creek above Trail Canyon near Cortez, CO	4	09371520	1993/08/01–2005/12/28	1,200	2.73	55.9	43.0	4,530
McElmo Creek below Cortez, CO	3	09371700	1972/10/01–1983/09/30	470	0.04	41.6	28.0	4,020
McElmo Creek near Colorado–Utah State line	1	09372000	1951/03/01–2005/12/28	1,220	0.08	50.1	37.9	20,000
McElmo Creek near Cortez, CO	5	09371500	1926/10/01–1929/09/30, 1940/10/01–1943/09/30, 1950/10/01–1954/09/30, 1982/01/01–1993/09/30	1,480	2.00	57.3	47.0	7,940
Mud Creek at State Highway 32, near Cortez, CO	6	09371492	1981/10/01–1986/09/30, 1993/08/01–2005/12/28	230	0.23	7.43	4.30	6,360
Mud Creek near Cortez, CO	7	09371495	1978/04/01–1981/09/30, 1983/10/01–1984/09/30	154	0.03	6.31	3.60	1,650
Navajo wash near Towaoc, CO	3	09371002	1986/10/01–1988/09/30, 1989/04/01–1994/09/30	100	0.33	8.59	6.15	2,740

region ranged from 0.03 ft³/s at site 7 to 6,950 ft³/s at site 17 (table 6).

Site 1, McElmo Creek near Colorado–Utah State line, is the farthest downstream site used to determine water quality for this report and is generally a good indicator of the quality of water discharging from the McElmo Creek basin (fig. 1). The maximum and minimum daily streamflows were 1,220 ft³/s and 0.08 ft³/s, respectively, over a period of record from March 1, 1951, through December 28, 2005. The mean and median daily streamflows for this period were 50.1 ft³/s and 37.9 ft³/s, respectively (table 6). Figure 7 shows the daily streamflow for site 1 and the water year annual total in acre-feet. The graphs show low daily and annual flows during the drought years 1977, 2002, and 2003.

The dominant pattern of daily streamflow in McElmo Creek consists of high flows in the spring as a result of snowmelt and runoff, followed by a decrease in streamflow throughout the irrigation season and then an increase in streamflow in the fall and winter as irrigation ceases and precipitation is more frequent. Streamflow patterns for tributaries to McElmo Creek are influenced substantially by irrigation and typically would be ephemeral if irrigation was not present in the region. However, because irrigation is present, streamflows typically increase during the snowmelt period and remain relatively high during the irrigation season, and then recede as irrigation ceases for the season.

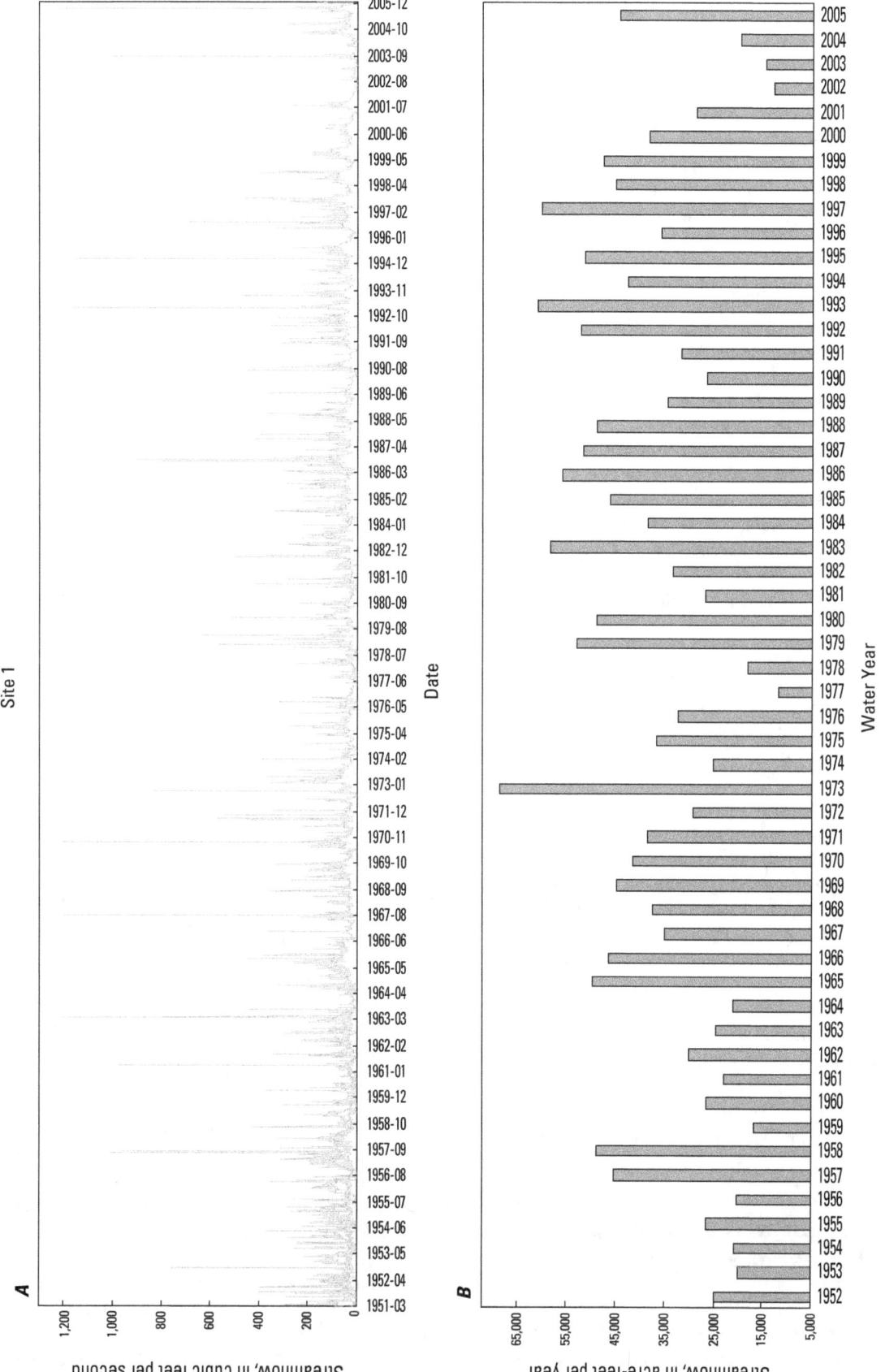

Figure 7. (*A*) Daily streamflow for site 1, McElmo Creek near Colorado–Utah State line, from March 1951 to December 2005. (*B*) Streamflow in acre-feet per year at site 1, McElmo Creek near Colorado–Utah State line, for water years 1952–2005.

Salinity

Salinity concentrations and loads for the McElmo Creek basin were estimated and summarized for watershed inputs and outputs. The daily mean salinity concentrations were calculated for each water year of the preperiod and postperiod to analyze the effects of salinity-control efforts associated with the Dolores Project. Salinity-concentration data contained annual daily mean summary statistics for the 7-year preperiod (water years 1978–1984) and the 7-year postperiod (water years 2000–2006). Preperiod and postperiod median values were compared between corresponding input and output sites in the basin.

Daily mean salinity concentrations are summarized in table 7 for the preperiod and the postperiod. The values in table 7 are represented in graphical form in figure 8 as box plots comparing the preperiod and postperiod for salinity concentration. The main inflow source of irrigation water to McPhee Reservoir and the McElmo Creek basin is monitored at site 17, Dolores River at Dolores, CO. Daily salinity concentrations for water in McPhee Reservoir outlet canals are very similar or identical to those for the Dolores River; therefore, concentration values from the Dolores River at Dolores were used to fill in any missing daily salinity values for the basin input canals.

Preperiod and postperiod salinity concentrations at selected sites in the McElmo Creek basin are compared in figure 8. Salinity concentrations decreased from the preperiod to the postperiod in the main basin outflow. The median salinity concentration for site 1 (main basin outflow) decreased from 2,210 mg/L per day in the preperiod to 2,110 mg/L per day in the postperiod. However, the median salinity concentration for site 6 (tributary outflow) increased from 3,370 mg/L per day in the preperiod to 3,710 mg/L per day in the postperiod. Salinity concentrations typically increased from the preperiod to the postperiod at inflow sites. Median salinity concentration increased from 178 mg/L per day during the preperiod at site 16 to 227 mg/L per day during the postperiod at site 15.

The reader is cautioned that the data represented above are not flow adjusted (normalized). Decreases or increases of streamflow could be associated with droughts or major precipitation events and could have an effect on salinity concentration. Non-flow-adjusted data were selected to be represented here to add insight to trends in salinity concentration during the study period.

Effect of Irrigation-Delivery and Salinity-Control Work by the Dolores Project

Salinity trend analysis (non-flow-adjusted) for the preperiod and postperiod indicates a change in salinity load after completion of the reservoir. Data analysis indicates the salinity load at site 1 was approximately 772,000 tons for the 7-year

preperiod (water years 1978–1984) (table 8). Navajo Wash (site 3) carried approximately 52,700 additional tons of salt out of the basin. The total salinity load exiting the McElmo Creek basin was about 824,700 tons during the preperiod. Inputs of salinity load to the watershed were calculated using data for sites 10, 13, and 14 combined; site 16; and site 18. Salinity load entering the basin at these sites was estimated to be about 82,700 tons, 77,100 tons, and 6,990 tons, respectively, during the preperiod. Therefore, the total salinity load entering the basin at inflow sites was about 167,000 tons during the preperiod. The difference between the inflow salinity load and the outflow salinity load indicates the number of tons of salt picked up within the basin. Therefore, the amount of salinity added in McElmo Creek basin was 657,700 tons during the preperiod (table 8).

Analysis of postperiod data indicates the salinity load leaving the McElmo Creek basin at site 1 was 475,000 tons over the 7-year period from 2000 through 2006. An additional 38,700 tons left the basin through Navajo Wash (site 3). The total salinity load exiting the basin during the postperiod was approximately 513,700 tons. Inflow sites for the postperiod were site 11, site 12, site 15, and site 18. The salinity load entering the basin at each of these sites were 7,900, 91,800, 136,000, and 4,560 tons, respectively, from 2000 to 2006. Total inflows of salinity load for the postperiod were 240,000 tons. Therefore, the total amount of salinity added within the basin during the postperiod was 273,700 tons (table 8), which is 384,000 tons less than during the preperiod. Figure 9 illustrates the preperiod and postperiod salinity loads together and allows for comparison of preperiod and postperiod loads at each site.

A summary of the water and salinity balance from the preperiod and the postperiod is shown in table 8. The percentage of change that occurred at each inflow site and outflow site from the 1978–1984 preperiod to the 2000–2006 postperiod also is shown. The amount of inflow increased from 909,000 acre-ft during the preperiod to 983,000 acre-ft during the postperiod. Outflows decreased from 298,000 acre-ft during the preperiod to 214,000 acre-ft during the postperiod. Typically, the inflows of salinity load were higher in the postperiod than they were in the preperiod. The outflows typically decreased in salinity load from the preperiod to the postperiod. Decreases in salinity load were as much as 38 percent at site 1 and 27 percent at site 3. Total salinity load, in tons per period, for inflow sites increased from 167,000 tons for the preperiod to 240,000 tons for the postperiod, which is a 44-percent increase in salinity load from inflow sites. The total salinity load, in tons per period, for outflow sites decreased from 824,700 tons during the preperiod to 513,700 tons during the postperiod, which is a 38-percent decrease in salinity load from the outflow sites (table 8).

The reader is cautioned that the decreases and increases in salinity load are not flow adjusted and are a function of the raw data. Therefore, seasonal and climatological effects are inherent in the analysis. Adjustments for wet years in the mid-1980s and drought years in 2002 and 2003 were not included

Table 7. Summary statistics for daily mean salinity concentration for selected sites in the McElmo Creek region from water years 1978–1984 (preperiod) and water years 2000–2006 (postperiod).

[Fig., figure; No. of obs, number of observations; Min, minimum value; Max, maximum value; Concentration, total dissolved solids concentration, not flow adjusted; mg/L, milligrams per liter; --, no data]

Site no. (fig. 1)	Site name	Daily salinity concentration, in mg/L											
		October 1977 through September 1984						October 1999 through September 2006					
		No. of obs	Min	25th percentile	Mean/Median	75th percentile	Max	No. of obs	Min	25th percentile	Mean/Median	75th percentile	Max
1	McElmo Creek near Colorado-Utah state line	2,557	560	1,610	2,200/2,210	2,711	4,390	2,557	655	1,360	2,030/2,110	2,610	3,500
6	Mud Creek at State Hwy 32 near Cortez, CO	2,192	212	2,160	3,450/3,370	4,590	7,620	2,557	280	1,330	3,370/3,710	5,030	10,200
15	Dolores Tunnel near Dolores, CO	--	--	--	--/--	--	--	2,557	75.5	177	225/227	283	427
16	Main Canal #1	2,042	72.8	127	190/178	255	322	--	--	--	--/--	--	--
17	Dolores River at Dolores, CO	2,557	73.0	145	204/208	270	322	2557	75.5	177	225/227	283	427

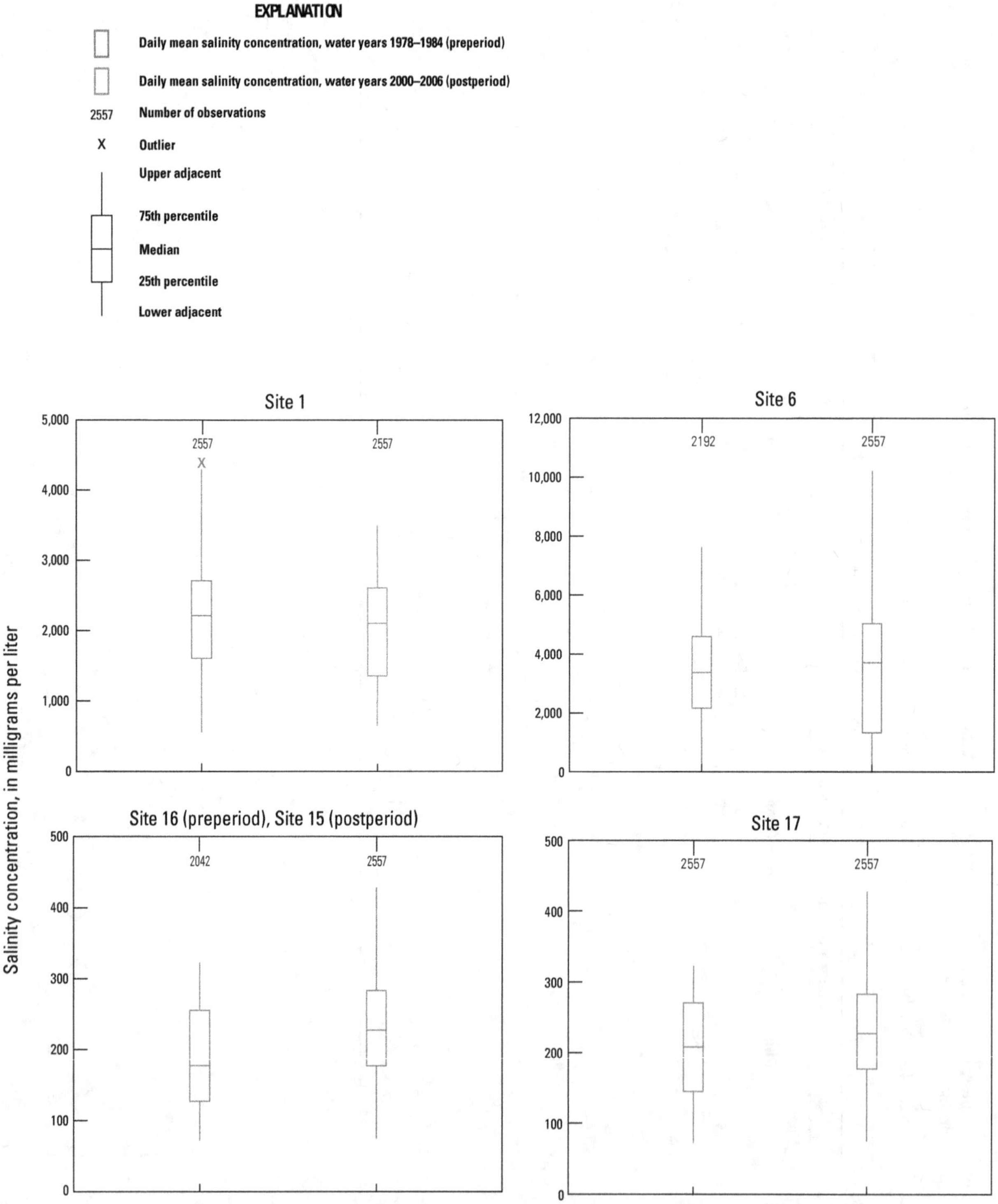

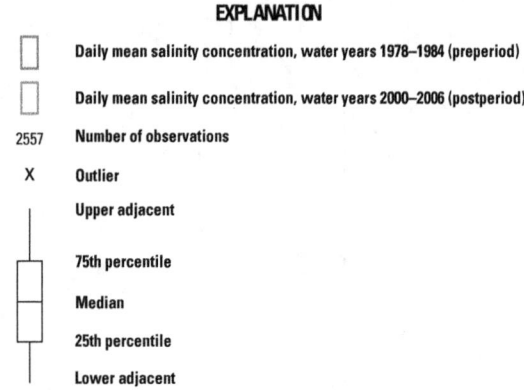

EXPLANATION
Daily mean salinity concentration, water years 1978–1984 (preperiod)
Daily mean salinity concentration, water years 2000–2006 (postperiod)
2557 Number of observations
X Outlier
Upper adjacent
75th percentile
Median
25th percentile
Lower adjacent
Salinity concentration, in milligrams per liter
Site 1
2557
2557
Site 6
2192
2557
Site 16 (preperiod), Site 15 (postperiod)
2042
2557
Site 17
2557
2557

Figure 8. Boxplots showing distribution of daily mean salinity concentrations at various sites in McElmo Creek basin, southwest Colorado.

Table 8.   Salinity balance with comparisons of preperiod and postperiod salinity loads for inflow and outflow sites.

[Study period: water years 1978–1984 preperiod; water years 2000–2006 postperiod; acre-feet, total acre-feet of discharge for 7-year period; tons per period, total tons of salt per 7-year period]

Site number (fig. 1)	Preperiod (1978-1984)			Postperiod (2000-2006)			Percent change	
	Discharge, in acre-feet/ period	Salinity load, in tons/period	Salinity load, in tons/acre-foot	Discharge, in acre-feet/period	Salinity load, in tons/period	Salinity load, in tons/ acre-foot	Tons per period (%)	Tons per acre-foot (%)
			Outflow sites					
1	277,000	772,000	2.78	198,000	475,000	2.40	-38	-14
3	21,100	52,700	2.50	16,000	38,700	2.42	-27	-3.2
Total	298,000	824,700	2.77	214,000	513,700	2.40	-38	-13
			Inflow sites					
10,13,14[1]	419,000	82,700	0.197	--	--	--	21[2]	30[2,3]
11	--	--	--	31,700	7,900	0.249		
12	--	--	--	351,000	91,800	0.262		
15	--	--	--	564,000	136,000	0.241	76[4]	36[4]
16	435,000	77,100	0.177	--	--	--		
18	55,200	6,990	0.127	36,000	4,560	0.127	-35	0.0
Total	909,000	167,000	0.184	983,000	240,000	0.244	44	32

[1]Combined data for three sites, Lone Pine Canal at Highway Bridge (site 10), U-Lateral Montezuma Valley Irrigation Company (site 13), and Main Canal #2 (site 14) into one input site.

[2]Sites 10, 13, and 14 represented the preperiod and sites 11 and 12 represented the postperiod.

[3]Postperiod tons per acre-feet used to determine percentage is the average value of sites 11 and 12 of 0.256 ton per acre-ft.

[4]Site 16 represented the preperiod and site 15 represented the postperiod.

in this analysis. Large fluctuations in the amount of flow entering and leaving the basin are indicated in table 6. Changing the flow regime can increase or decrease the salinity that is transported through a system. To more clearly understand the amount of salinity load change that occurred from the preperiod to the postperiod, the data need to be flow adjusted to compensate for as many seasonal and climatological effects as possible.

Flow-Adjusted SalinityTrends

Flow-adjusted salinity trends in McElmo Creek basin were analyzed by using output from S-LOADEST and residual plots with a LOWESS noise-reduction algorithm. S-LOADEST load estimations for site 1 indicate a decrease in annual salinity load of 39,800 tons (32 percent) from water year 1978 through water year 2006, which is an average decrease of 1,370 tons per year for the 29-year period (fig. 10A, table 9). Annual salinity-load estimates for site 6 indicate a decrease of about 7,300 tons (36 percent) from water year 1982 through water year 2006, which is an average decrease of 292 tons per year for the 25-year period. Site 17 was selected to represent a background site that is not affected by the Dolores Project. Annual salinity-load estimations for site 17 indicate a decrease of about 8,600 tons (12 percent) from water year 1978 through

water year 2006, which is an average of 297 tons per year for the 29-year period (fig. 10B, table 9). The trend in load at site 17 was considered to be representative of a natural trend in the region due to factors that were outside the scope of this study. The natural trend estimated at site 17 may also be present at site 1 and site 6, reducing the actual trend associated with salinity-control efforts. Site 1 represents the results of salinity control measures within the basin and the salinity-load trend basinwide. A more detailed summary of salinity trend data estimated by S-LOADEST can be found in table 9 and Appendix 1.1–1.6.

Analysis of partial residual plots with a LOWESS curve and timeline of events indicates the changes in salinity concentration over time. Figures 10A and 11 show salinity concentration decreases occurring in the late 1980s and early 1990s. Salinity data were analyzed to estimate the salinity load change during this period, which is also associated with salinity-control efforts in the basin. Using S-LOADEST to calculate loads at site 1 for water years 1989–2006, a decrease of approximately 21,700 tons (21 percent) was estimated, which is an average decrease of 1,210 tons per year for the 18-year period (table 10) and represents 55 percent of the total trend during the water years 1978–2006 period (table 9). Estimates for site 6 for water years 1990–2006 indicate a decrease in salinity load of about 4,000 tons (25 percent), which is an

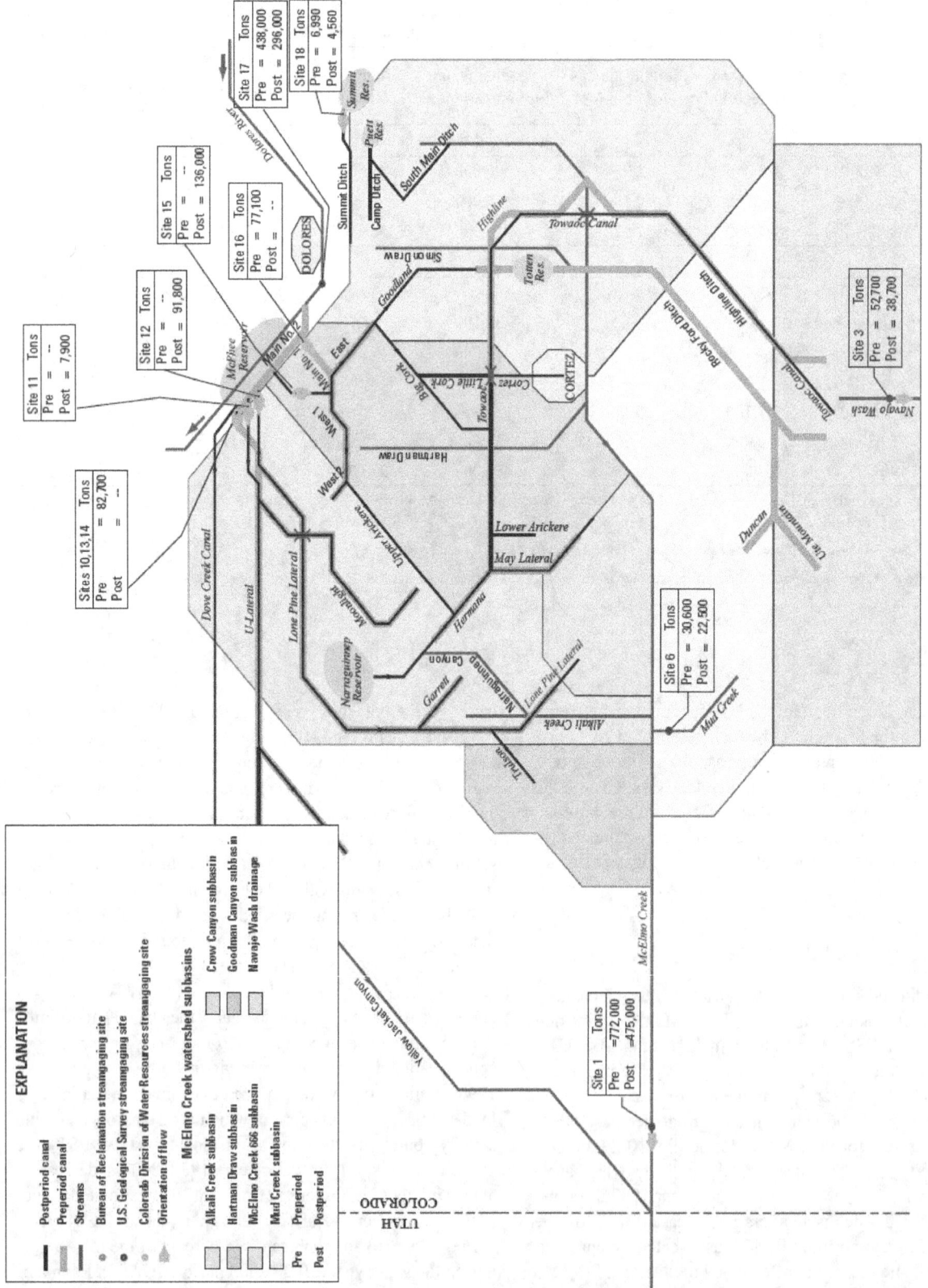

Figure 9. Pipe diagram comparing non-flow-adjusted salinity load in tons from water years 1978–1984 (preperiod) to salinity load in tons from water years 2000–2006 (postperiod) at selected sites in the McElmo Creek basin area, southwest Colorado.

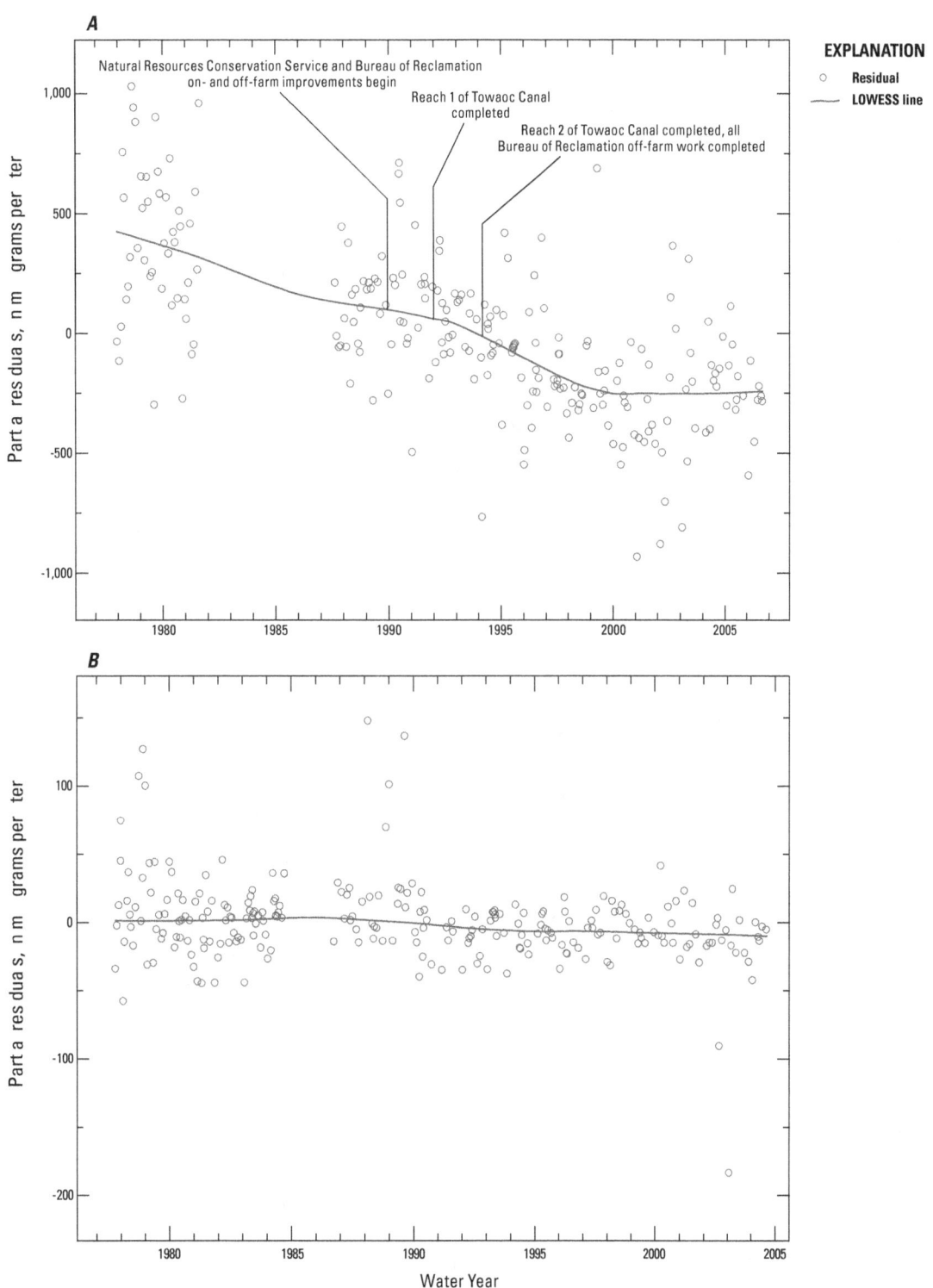

Figure 10.   Partial residual plot of salinity concentration with LOWESS curve at (*A*) McElmo Creek near Colorado–Utah State line (site 1) and (*B*) Dolores River at Dolores, Colorado (site 17).

Table 9.   Salinity-load estimates and flow-adjusted trend-analysis summary for water years 1978–2006.

[Numbers determined using S-LOADEST software (Insightful Corp., 2005a); 95th percent confidence interval, upper and lower limits; tons/day, tons per day; SEP, standard error of prediction; Annual load, in tons; Average change in annual load, in tons per year (tons/yr); Δ, change]

| Water year | Daily mean salinity load (tons/day) | Variance (tons/day) | 95-percent confidence interval | | SEP (tons/day) | Annual load (tons) | Percent change | Average change in annual load (tons/yr) |
			Lower limit (tons/day)	Upper limit (tons/day)				
			Site 1					
1978	344	35.4	331	356	6.39	125,000	--	--
2006	233	14.1	225	241	4.07	85,200	--	--
					Δ annual load=	−39,800	−32	−1,370
			Site 6					
1982	55.1	1.00	52.9	57.3	1.12	20,100	--	--
2006	35.0	0.70	33.3	36.7	0.90	12,800	--	--
					Δ annual load=	−7,300	−36	−292
			Site 17					
1978	192	29.9	181	204	5.82	70,000	--	--
2006	168	31.5	157	180	5.88	61,400	--	--
					Δ annual load=	−8,600	−12	−297

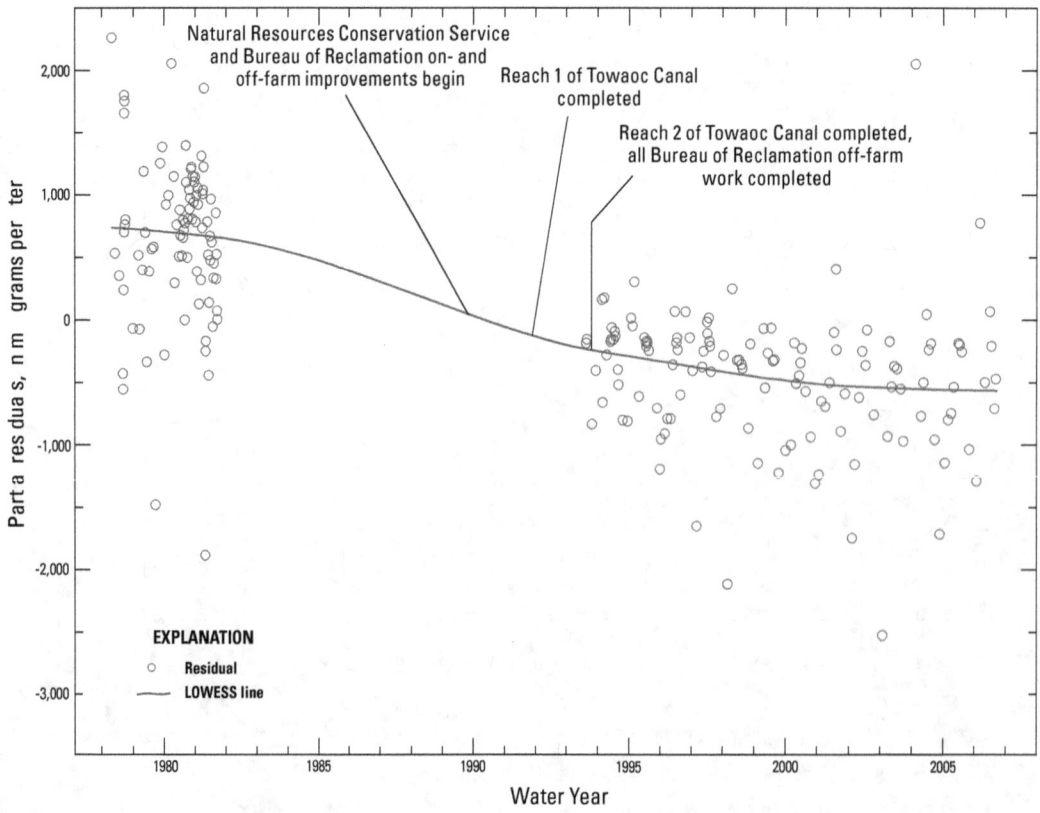

Figure 11.   Partial residual plot of salinity concentrations with LOWESS curve of Mud Creek at State Highway 32 near Cortez, Colorado (site 6).

Table 10.　Salinity load estimates and flow-adjusted trend analysis summary for water years 1989–2006.

[Numbers determined using S-LOADEST software (Insightful Corp., 2005a); 95th percent confidence interval, upper and lower limits; tons/day, tons per day; SEP, standard error of prediction; Annual load, in tons; Average change in annual load, in tons per year (tons/yr); Δ, change]

| Water year | Daily mean salinity load (tons/day) | Variance (tons/day) | 95-percent confidence interval | | SEP (tons/day) | Annual load (tons) | Percent change | Average change in annual load (tons/yr) |
			Lower limit (tons/day)	Upper limit (tons/day)				
				Site 1				
1989	280	7.44	273	286	3.33	102,000		--
2006	220	12.7	213	228	3.87	80,300		--
				Δ annual load=		−21,700	−21	−1,210
				Site 6				
1990	43.6	0.40	42.2	45.1	0.76	15,900		--
2006	32.6	0.53	31.1	34.2	0.79	11,900		--
				Δ annual load=		−4,000	−25	−235
				Site 17				
1989	146	4.11	141	150	2.49	53,100		--
2006	134	8.81	128	141	3.25	49,000		--
				Δ annual load=		−4,100	−8.7	−228

average of 235 tons per year, for the 17-year period from 1990–2006 (table 10) and represents 55 percent of the total salinity load reduction for the water years 1982–2006 period (table 9). A detailed summary of load estimations for water years 1989–2006 is provided in table 10.

The decrease in salinity load at site 1 was compared to estimations of salinity load reduction from salinity control by the USBR and Natural Resources Conservation Service (NRCS). The results showed a larger decrease in salinity than was anticipated by the USBR or the NRCS in their salinity-reduction estimates. Estimates from the Dolores Project Report included a reduction of 32,000 tons per year from salinity control modifications associated with the Dolores Project (Bureau of Reclamation, 1988). The NRCS estimated an additional reduction of 18,000 tons per year for its contributions to on-farm and off-farm improvements (Frank Riggle, oral commun., 2009). Of this additional reduction, NRCS records estimate that 13,000 tons per year are attributed to their on-farm improvement, including sprinkler systems and on-farm piping projects, and an estimated 5,000 tons per year are attributed by the NRCS to off-farm improvements, including improvements to canals and the off-farm delivery system (Frank Riggle, oral commun., 2009) (table 11). The total estimated salinity-load reduction claimed by both the USBR and the NRCS is approximately 50,000 tons per year from water years 1978 to 2006 (table 11). The reductions offset the estimated increase of approximately 50,650 tons per year associated with the Dolores Project Plan (Bureau of Reclamation,

1988), resulting in approximately no net change (650 tons) in annual salinity load.

Analysis of the water-quality data for site 1 indicates that a large part of the downward trend in salinity load that occurred was not claimed by either the NRCS or the USBR. An additional reduction in salinity load of 39,150 tons is present in the salinity load trend for water years 1978–2006 at site 1 (tables 9 and 11).

Trend Analysis in the Mud Creek Subbasin

The Mud Creek subbasin comprises 22,051 acres of the McElmo Creek basin and contains 3,425 acres of irrigated lands watered from the Towaoc Canal (fig. 3). Initial analysis of the Mud Creek subbasin by the USGS indicated it might be a good candidate for determining on-farm and off-farm loads from a Mancos Shale setting because the subbasin contains predominantly Mancos Shale or Mancos Shale-derived soils (fig. 5). Analysis of the data and additional information supplied by the NRCS indicates that separation of on-farm and off-farm salinity loads was not possible. Salinity-control measures implemented by the NRCS and the USBR coincide with each other, making estimation of on-farm or off-farm loads unfeasible with the dataset that is available. The Mud Creek subbasin was one of the first areas where salinity-control measures were implemented by the NRCS. Sprinkler systems for 1,236 acres were improved during 1990–1994, and the NRCS

Table 11.   Summary of salinity-load reductions and trend analysis at site 1 for water years 1978–2006.

[Unclaimed trend determined using S-LOADEST software (Insightful Corp., 2005a); USBR, Bureau of Reclamation; NRCS, Natural Resources Conservation Service; --, no data]

	Estimated increase, tons	Actual increase, tons	Estimated decrease, tons	Claimed decrease, tons	Unclaimed trend, tons
Dolores Project Report	50,650	Unknown	--	--	--
USBR off-farm	--	--	−32,000	−32,000	--
NRCS on-farm	--	--	--	−13,000	--
NRCS off-farm	--	--	--	−5,000	--
Total decrease	--	--	--	−50,000	--
Total trend	--	--	--	650	--
S-LOADEST trend	--	--	--	--	−39,150[1]

[1] The unclaimed trend was calculated by subtracting the total trend in claimed decrease (650 tons) from the change in annual load at site 1 in table 9 (39,800 tons).

estimated salt reduction of 1,609 tons per year from this work. Additional improvements included 36,979 feet of on- and off-farm canals and laterals that were lined or piped, resulting in a predicted reduction of 560 tons of salinity per year (Frank Riggle, oral commun., 2009).

Data analysis of the Mud Creek subbasin indicates a downward trend of salinity concentration and load beginning shortly after NRCS and USBR improvements began on the delivery canals and water delivery systems in 1990. Reductions in salinity concentrations were seen after the first and second sections of the Towaoc Canal were lined by the USBR in 1992 and 1994 (fig. 11). Reductions from 1994 through 2006 are assumed to be a result of NRCS improvements both on-farm and off-farm. Separation of on- and off-farm trends is difficult due to the timing of improvements. Estimated salinity loads from S-LOADEST calculations indicate an estimated reduction of 7,300 tons in the Mud Creek subbasin from water year 1982 through water year 2006 (table 9), which is an average of 292 tons per year. S-LOADEST estimations for water year 1990 through water year 2006 indicate a downward trend of 4,000 tons, which is an average of 235 tons per year and represents 55 percent of the water years 1982 to 2006 trend (table 10).

Natural Salinity in McElmo Creek Basin

Based on historical accounts from the town of Cortez, Colo., it was determined that McElmo Creek was not a perennial stream and was probably ephemeral in nature. Historical records indicate that the city of Cortez was established in late 1886 to supply housing for the Montezuma Valley Water Supply Company employees who were hired to build tunnels, ditches, and laterals that were required to divert water from the Dolores River into Montezuma Valley. The water supply for the settlement was hauled from a spring 2 miles from town; later, a well, which eventually went dry, was dug in the center

of town (City of Cortez, 2008). This indicated that McElmo Creek was not a reliable source of water year round and that base flow was not adequate to maintain flows in the creek.

Historical flows in McElmo Creek were assumed to be a result of snowmelt and high-intensity rainstorms, similar to the flow regime of many ephemeral streams in semiarid to arid environments. Analysis of streamflow hydrographs of average precipitation years in the basin indicated that between 30 and 40 percent of the annual flow in McElmo Creek is a result of high-intensity precipitation and snowmelt. Geologic conditions in the basin are conducive to rapid-runoff conditions that create spikes in streamflow. Hydrograph analysis on a year-by-year basis indicates that late-summer to early-fall high-intensity monsoonal storms create streamflow that can peak rapidly at more than 1,000 ft^3/s, then recede in a matter of days. Historically, these events would have dominated the streamflow regime. The intensity of such storms is documented in a June 10, 1911, event that resulted in a rapid increase in streamflow in McElmo Creek that completely washed away orchards and irrigation flumes and laterals and incised a new channel within McElmo Canyon (City of Cortez, 2008).

Because on- and off-farm salinity loads could not be determined separately in the Mud Creek subbasin, an alternative approach was taken to estimate the natural salinity load for McElmo Creek basin. The most concentrated salts are typically in areas where marine sedimentary deposits are present because dissolved solids precipitated to form salts as the ancient marine bodies evaporated. In order to determine a natural salinity load from McElmo Creek basin, all influences of irrigation, industry, and municipalities were removed, resulting in a historical, natural setting herein referred to as the historic period.

The flow regime for the historic period in McElmo Creek was estimated using a water-budget analysis of the basin. Evapotranspiration (ET) rates for the irrigated land and the nonirrigated land were both estimated using the NRCS

Blanney-Criddle method outlined in Ward and Trimble (2004). Crop coefficients for ET estimations were applied to a reference ET to estimate the volume of ET from each crop type. The crop coefficients used were (0.90) for alfalfa and (0.85) for grass pasture (Allen and others, 1998). The total water volume obtained from calculating the ET rate for irrigation was removed from the volume of water diverted into McElmo Creek basin from canals (983,000 acre-ft) for irrigation for the 7-year postperiod. Using this method it was estimated that 86 percent of the diverted water for irrigation was consumed by crops within the basin. Therefore, an estimated 845,000 acre-ft of water was consumed by crops and did not return to creeks as streamflow. The remaining 138,000 acre-ft that was not consumed was subtracted from the postperiod outflow of 214,000 acre-ft. The remaining 76,200 acre-ft, or 10,900 acre-ft per year for the 7-year postperiod, was assumed to represent a historical flow condition without the influence of diverted water for irrigation. The period from water year 2000 to 2006 only represented 80 percent of the long-term precipitation average; therefore, the historical streamflow could be as much as 20 percent more than the estimated value of 76,200 acre-ft.

Historical natural salinity loads were estimated using measured concentrations from natural surface-water sites, when possible, and wells. Sites were selected from sandstone and shale rock types in areas not affected by irrigation. Average TDS concentrations for each type of rock were used to estimate salinity loads. Most surface-water sites used to estimate a natural TDS concentration were springs. An average TDS value for water from sandstones in the basin was 350 mg/L, and the average for water from shale was 4,000 mg/L. The historical flow of 10,900 acre-ft per year is equivalent to 15.1 cubic feet per second (ft³/s) and was entered into equation 1 along with the average TDS concentration for each rock type. The area of McElmo Creek basin that is underlain by sandstone is 129,000 acres, which is 56 percent of the basin and Mancos shale underlies 101,000 acres, which is 44 percent of the basin. Salinity loads for each rock type were estimated using equation 1 by taking the proportion of flow for each rock type, based on percentage of the basin, and the respective average TDS value (table 12).

Natural salinity loads in McElmo Creek were estimated to be 29,100 tons per year for concentrations based on natural spring water (table 12). This is 43 percent of the 67,900 tons per year salinity load that was calculated for the postperiod (water years 2000–2006; table 8). The reported natural loads are considered estimates, and variation from year to year is expected. Salinity loads and concentrations are dependent on the locality and geologic conditions of the area affected by storms. Salt crusts on the surface of the soil in Mancos Shale areas can create an increase in concentration during rainstorms, which tapers off after the initial flushing. Reported salinity loads are an estimated average based on an estimated average concentration and may not accurately reflect these flushing events.

Summary

The Colorado Salinity Control Act, Public Law 93–320, June 24, 1974, was implemented to enhance and protect the quality of water in the Colorado River. Title II of the Colorado Salinity Control Act authorized the investigation and implementation of control measures for selected salinity-control units, including the McElmo Creek basin in Montezuma County, southwestern Colorado. Salinity is a concern in the McElmo Creek region of the Upper Colorado River Basin. Additional irrigation water storage, due to the development of McPhee Reservoir as part of the Dolores Project in the early 1980s, lengthened the irrigation season, which potentially allowed for increases in salinity to McElmo Creek and its tributaries.

Salinity-control projects such as irrigation and water-delivery system improvements have been implemented in the McElmo Creek basin to reduce the overall salinity load to McElmo Creek. The Dolores Project, located in the McElmo Creek salinity-control unit, was developed to help support the agricultural industry, which farms about 62,000 acres of irrigated land in the area. To offset the increase of salinity due to the increased irrigation season and to maintain crop productivity, salinity-control features were completed as part of the Dolores Project.

Interest in understanding water and salt budgets and also the effectiveness of salinity-control efforts since the construction of McPhee Reservoir has resulted in a network of water-quality monitoring sites, predominantly operated by the U.S.

Table 12. Historical salinity load summary for McElmo Creek basin, southwest Colorado.

[USBR, Bureau of Reclamation; TDS, total dissolved solids; mg/L, milligram per liter; ft³/s, cubic feet per second; --, not applicable]

Rock type	Area (acres)	Average TDS concentration (mg/L)	Average discharge (ft³/s)	Average salinity load, (tons/year)
Sandstone	129,000	350	8.45	2,900
Mancos Shale	101,000	4,000	6.65	26,200
Total	230,000	--	15.1	29,100

Geological Survey (USGS) and Colorado Division of Water Resources (CDWR). Comparisons of the salinity loads exiting the basin during the preperiod (water years 1978–1984) and postperiod (water years 2000–2006) allows insight to the effectiveness of salinity-control features that were implemented and whether additional control is needed.

Salinity-control features included in the Dolores Project were designed to help reduce and offset the salinity loading that resulted from increased water usage and longer irrigation seasons. According to revised estimates by the Bureau of Reclamation (USBR) for the 1977 Dolores Project Definite Plan Report, there would be 43,150 tons per year of salt would enter McElmo Creek from project lands and canals. Realignment of the Towaoc Canal would add another 7,500 tons per year, for a total of 50,650 tons/year, as a result of plan development. Salinity-control features, including the realignment of the Towaoc Canal, and project modifications were estimated to reduce the salinity load by 32,000 tons per year. Therefore, an estimated increase of 18,650 tons per year would be the resulting salinity load, not including any on-farm irrigation controls for reducing salinity loading.

The streamflow regime of McElmo Creek is based largely on seasonal moisture patterns, augmented by regulated releases from Summit Reservoir and McPhee Reservoir. Variations in flow regime affect the salinity load; therefore, variations between daily salinity loads are common.

Preperiod and postperiod salinity concentrations at selected sites in the McElmo Creek basin were compared. The median salinity concentration for site 1 (main basin outflow) decreased from 2,210 mg/L per day in the preperiod to 2,110 mg/L per day in the postperiod. The median salinity concentration for site 6 (tributary basin outflow) increased from 3,370 mg/L per day in the preperiod to 3,710 mg/L per day in the postperiod. Salinity concentrations typically increased from the preperiod to the postperiod at inflow sites. Salinity concentrations increased from 178 mg/L per day during the preperiod at site 16 to 227 mg/L per day during the postperiod at site 15.

Non-flow-adjusted salinity trend analysis for the preperiod and postperiod indicates a change in salinity load after completion of the reservoir. Data analysis indicates the preperiod (water years 1978–1984) salinity load at site 1 was approximately 772,000 tons for the 7-year period. Navajo Wash (site 3) carried approximately 52,700 additional tons of salt out of the basin. The total salinity load exiting the McElmo Creek basin was about 824,700 tons during the preperiod. Inputs of salinity load to the watershed were calculated using data for sites 10, 13, and 14 combined; site 16; and site 18. Salinity load entering the basin at these sites was estimated to be about 82,700 tons, 77,100 tons, and 6,990 tons, respectively, during the preperiod. Therefore, the total salinity load entering the basin at inflow sites was about 167,000 tons during the preperiod. The difference between the inflow salinity load and the outflow salinity load indicates the number of tons of salt picked up within the basin. Therefore, the amount of salinity picked up in McElmo Creek basin is 657,700 tons for the period 1978–1984.

Analysis of postperiod data indicates the salinity load leaving the McElmo Creek basin at site 1 was 475,000 tons over the 7-year period from 2000 through 2006. An additional 38,700 tons left the basin through Navajo Wash (site 3). The total salinity load exiting the basin during the postperiod was approximately 513,700 tons. Inflow sites for the postperiod were site 11, site 12, site 15, and site 18. The salinity loads entering the basin at each of these sites were 7,900, 91,800, 136,000, and 4,560 tons, respectively, from 2000 to 2006. Total inflow of salinity load for the postperiod was 240,000 tons. Therefore, the total amount of salt picked up within the basin during the postperiod was 273,700 tons, which is 384,000 tons less than during the preperiod.

Flow-adjusted salinity trends in McElmo Creek basin were analyzed by using output from S-LOADEST and residual plots with a LOWESS noise-reduction algorithm. S-LOADEST load estimations for site 1 indicate a decrease in salinity load by 39,800 tons from water year 1978 through water year 2006, which is an average decrease of 1,370 tons per year for the 29-year period. Annual-load estimates for site 6 indicate a decrease of about 7,300 tons from water year 1982 through water year 2006, which is an average decrease of 292 tons per year for the 25-year period. Site 17 was selected to represent a background site that is not affected by the Dolores Project. Annual-load estimates for site 17 indicate a decrease of about 8,600 tons from water year 1978 through water year 2006, which is an average decrease of 297 tons per year for the 29-year period. The trend in load at site 17 was considered to represent the natural background trend in the region.

The decrease in salinity trend at site 1 was compared to estimations of salinity load reduction from salinity control by the USBR and Natural Resources Conservation Service (NRCS). The results showed an excess decrease in salinity that was not claimed by the USBR or the NRCS in their salinity reduction estimates. Estimates from the Dolores Report included a reduction of 32,000 tons per year from salinity-control modifications associated with the Dolores Project. The NRCS estimated an additional reduction of 18,000 tons per year in 2006 for its contributions to on-farm and off-farm improvements. The total estimated salinity load reduction claimed by both the USBR and the NRCS is approximately 50,000 tons per year from water year 1978 through water year 2006. Analysis of the water-quality data at site 1 indicates that a large part of the downward trend in salinity load that occurred was not claimed by either the NRCS or the USBR. An additional reduction in salinity load of 39,150 tons per year is present in the salinity load trend at site 1.

Calculation of the historical flow regime in McElmo Creek was done using a water-budget analysis of the basin. Using this method it was estimated that 86 percent of the diverted water for irrigation during the postperiod was consumed by crops within the basin; therefore, an estimated 845,000 acre-ft of water is consumed by crops and did not return to the creek as streamflow. The remaining

76,000 acre-ft, or 10,900 acre-ft per year for the 7-year post-period, was assumed to represent the historical flow condition without the influence of diverted water for irrigation.

Average TDS concentrations for water from sandstone and shale in the area were used to estimate natural salinity loads. Most surface-water sites used to estimate a natural TDS concentration were springs. An average TDS value for water from sandstones in the basin was 350 mg/L, and the average value for water from shale was 4,000 mg/L. The historical flow of 10,900 acre-ft per year was converted to 15.1 cubic feet per second. Natural salinity loads in McElmo Creek were estimated to be 29,100 tons per year for concentrations based on natural spring water. This is 43 percent of the load that was calculated for the postperiod. Estimated natural loads may be widely variable with changes from year to year.

Acknowledgments

The authors of this report thank the following individuals. Thanks to Frank Riggle (Natural Resources Conservation Service) for supplying insight on agricultural practices and off-farm data; Stan Powers (Bureau of Reclamation) for providing data, insight, and knowledge throughout the report; Robert Wilson (formerly of the U.S. Geological Survey) for data collection; Cory Williams (U.S. Geological Survey) for support throughout the project and statistical insight; David Mau (U.S. Geological Survey) and Katharine Foster (U.S. Geological Survey) for providing technical reviews.

References Cited

Allen, R.G., Pereira, L.S., Raes, D., and Smith, M., 1998, Crop evapotranspiration—Guidelines for computing crop water coefficients: Rome, United Nations Food and Agriculture Organization Irrigation and Drainage Paper no. 56, 300 p.

Bureau of Reclamation, 1988, Dolores Project Colorado: Supplement to definite plan report, Appendix B, Water Supply/Hydrosalinity, 131 p.

Bureau of Reclamation, 2003, Quality of water—Colorado River Basin: U.S. Department of the Interior Progress Report no. 21, 89 p.

Bureau of Reclamation, 2008, Dolores Project—Project data: Information available on the Web, accessed June 25, 2008, at *http://www.usbr.gov/projects/Project.jsp?proj_Name=Dolores+Project*.

City of Cortez, 2008, History of Cortez: Information available on the Web, accessed January 27, 2008 at *http://www.cityofcortez.com/government/mayor_city_council/advisory_boards/historic_preservation/history_cortez*.

Cohn, T.A., 2005, Estimating contaminant loads in rivers—An application of adjusted maximum likelihood to type 1 censored data: Water Resources Research, v. 41, 13 p.

Cohn, T.A., Caulder, D.L., Gilroy, E.J., Zynjuk, L.D., and Summers, R.M., 1992, The validity of a simple statistical model for estimating fluvial constituent loads—An empirical study involving nutrient loads entering Chesapeake Bay: Water Resources Research, v. 28, no. 9, p. 2353–2363.

Cohn, T.A., Delong, L.L., Gilroy, E.J., Hirsch, R.M., and Wells, D.K., 1989, Estimating constituent loads: Water Resources Research, v. 25, no. 5, p. 937–942.

Driver, N.E., and Tasker, G.D., 1990, Techniques for estimation or storm runoff loads, volumes, and selected constituent concentrations in urban watersheds in the United States: U.S. Geological Survey Water-Supply Paper 2363, 44 p.

Duan, Naihua, 1983, Smearing estimate—A nonparametric retransformation method: Journal of the American Statistical Association, v. 78, no. 383, p. 605–610.

Garrels, R.M., and Thompson, M.E., 1962, A chemical model for seawater at 25°C and one atmosphere total pressure: American Journal of Science, v. 260, p. 57–66.

Helsel, D.R., and Hirsch, R.M., 2002, Statistical methods in water resources: U.S. Geological Survey Techniques of Water-Resource Investigations, book 4, chap. A3, 510 p.

Hem, J.D., 1959, Study and interpretation of the chemical characteristics of natural water: U.S. Geological Survey Water-Supply Paper 1473, 269 p.

Hem, J.D., 1985, Study and interpretation of the chemical characteristics of natural water (3d ed.): U.S. Geological Survey Water-Supply Paper 2254, 72 p.

Hirsch, Robert M., 1982, A comparison of four streamflow record extension techniques: Water Resource Research, v. 18, no. 4 p. 1081–1088.

Insightful Corp., 2005a, S-PLUS 7.0 software: Seattle, Washington, Insightful Corporation.

Insightful Corp., 2005b, S-PLUS 7.0 for Windows—Users guide: Seattle, Washington, Insightful Corporation.

Iorns, W.V., Hembree, C.H., and Oakland, G.L., 1965, Water resources of the upper Colorado River Basin—Technical report: U.S. Geological Survey Professional Paper 441, 40 p.

Karlinger, M.R., and Troutman, B.M., 1985, Error bounds in cascading regressions: Mathematical Geology, v. 17, no. 3, p. 287–295.

Kircher, J.E., Dinicola, R.S., and Middelburg, R.F., 1984, Trend analysis of salt load and evaluation of the frequency of water-quality measurements for the Gunnison, the Colorado, and the Dolores Rivers in Colorado and Utah: U.S. Geological Survey Water-Resources Investigations Report 84–4048, 69 p.

Laronne, J.B., 1977, Dissolution potential of superficial Mancos Shale and alluvium: Fort Collins, Colorado State University, Ph.D. dissertation, 128 p.

Likes, Jiri, 1980, Variance of the MVUE for lognormal variance: Technometrics, v. 22 no. 2, p. 253–258.

Mills, Ian, Cvitas, T., Homann, K., Kallay, N., and Kuchitsu, K., 1993, Quantities, units and symbols in physical chemistry (2d ed.): Cambridge, International Union of Pure and Applied Chemistry, Blackwell Science, 165 p.

Runkel, R.L., Crawford, C.G., and Cohn, T.A., 2004, Load estimator (LOADEST)—A fortran program for estimating constituent loads in streams and rivers: U.S. Geological Survey Techniques and Methods, book 4, chap. A5, 69 p.

Techni Graphics Systems, Inc., 2004, Colorado Decision Support System 2000 Irrigated Parcels, accessed June 10th, 2006 at *http://cdss.state.co.us/DNN/GIS/tabid/67/Default. aspx.*

TIBCO, 2008, Spotfire S+® 8.1 for Windows® user's guide: TIBCO Software Inc., 2008, 572 p.

Tweto, Ogden, compiler, 1979, Geologic map of Colorado: U.S. Geologic Survey Map, scale 1:500,000.

U.S. Census Bureau, 2008, Population finder: Information available on Web, accessed September 17, 2008, at *http://www.census.gov/.*

U.S. Geological Survey Geographic Names Information System, 2008, Query form for the United States and its Territories: Information available on the Web, accessed September 15, 2008, at *http://geonames.usgs.gov/pls/ gnispublic.*

U.S. Geological Survey, variously dated, National field manual for the collection of water quality data in chap. A1–A9 of U.S. Geological Survey Techniques of Water-Resources Investigations, book 9, available online at *http://pubs.water.usgs.gov/twri9A.*

Ward, A.D., and Trimble, S.W., 2004, Environmental hydrology, 2d ed.: New York, CRC Press, 475 p.

Western Regional Climate Center, 2008, Colorado historical climate information: Information available on the Web, accessed September 15, 2008, at *http://www.wrcc.dri.edu/ CLIMATEDATA.html.*

Appendix: S-LOADEST Salinity Load Output Tables

Table 13.   S-LOADEST salinity load output[1] for site 1 from water year 1978 to water year 2006.

[Flux, salinity load in tons per day; Variance, the variability of flux in tons per day; Lower 95, lower limit of the 95th percentile confidence interval; Upper 95, upper limit of the 95th percentile confidence interval; SEP, standard error of flux prediction, in tons per day; N, number of days; Load, salinity load in tons per month]

Date	Flux	Variance	Lower 95	Upper 95	SEP	N	Load
			Monthly loads				
October 1977	403.9299	74.94589	379.8493	429.1214	12.57076	31	12,521.83
November 1977	390.7933	70.89384	367.2474	415.4375	12.29472	30	11,723.8
December 1977	325.6313	48.63212	306.2159	345.9425	10.13539	31	10,094.57
January 1978	312.1987	42.56686	293.8089	331.4264	9.59728	31	9,678.161
February 1978	425.8318	80.00632	399.5692	453.35	13.72116	28	11,923.29
March 1978	443.9319	90.8131	417.1231	471.9943	13.99927	30	13,317.96
April 1978	273.3916	32.52956	256.9087	290.644	8.606882	30	8,201.748
May 1978	229.2371	22.80389	215.6002	243.5019	7.118534	31	7,106.352
June 1978	268.7643	30.9509	252.8501	285.4075	8.306329	30	8,062.93
July 1978	287.3496	34.21494	270.5781	304.8779	8.750827	31	8,907.838
August 1978	351.6313	50.74442	331.1736	373.0091	10.6734	31	10,900.57
September 1978	420.9147	74.33005	396.0191	446.9494	12.99379	30	12,627.44
October 2005	281.5956	28.37686	265.679	298.2067	8.298664	32	9,011.058
November 2005	263.1313	30.65655	247.4459	279.5403	8.188206	30	7,893.939
December 2005	219.254	21.89784	206.2019	232.9074	6.813361	31	6,796.874
January 2006	210.2083	19.69931	197.7682	223.218	6.492987	31	6,516.458
February 2006	286.7165	38.6259	268.7972	305.5044	9.365183	28	8,028.062
March 2006	298.4566	42.13944	280.4759	317.276	9.388822	31	9,252.154
April 2006	180.5848	12.64101	169.9494	191.7046	5.550392	30	5,417.543
May 2006	157.561	8.552516	148.6265	166.8867	4.658646	31	4,884.391
June 2006	180.4993	10.66459	170.3798	191.0566	5.275177	30	5,414.978
July 2006	196.9584	12.17798	186.0809	208.2992	5.668438	31	6,105.71
August 2006	235.2241	18.49989	222.105	248.9078	6.838073	31	7,291.948
September 2006	287.6894	32.03042	270.9496	305.1821	8.733646	30	8,630.681
			Annual loads				
Water year 1978	343.5892	35.40149	331.238	356.2779	6.38797	364	125,066.5
Water year 2006	232.9065	14.10996	225.024	240.9915	4.073478	366	85,243.8

[1] Raw output data from S-LOADEST (Insightful Corp., 2005a), not adjusted to significant figures.

Table 14. S-LOADEST salinity load output[1] for site 1 from water year 1989 to water year 2006.

[Flux, salinity load in tons per day; Variance, the variability of flux in tons per day; Lower 95, lower limit of the 95th percentile confidence interval; Upper 95, upper limit of the 95th percentile confidence interval; SEP, standard error of flux prediction, in tons per day; N, number of days; Load, salinity load in tons per month]

Date	Flux	Variance	Lower 95	Upper 95	SEP	N	Load
			Monthly loads				
October 1988	376.3423	35.11645	356.3983	397.1001	10.38397	31	11,666.61
November 1988	332.9195	29.39587	314.9106	351.6792	9.380554	30	9,987.586
December 1988	253.4859	17.43116	239.8919	267.6416	7.07962	31	7,858.064
January 1989	259.3466	16.81278	245.6133	273.6398	7.150216	31	8,039.746
February 1989	346.5395	30.7163	327.1118	366.8078	10.12748	28	9,703.107
March 1989	311.406	24.15163	294.6305	328.8778	8.737295	31	9,653.586
April 1989	172.4141	6.433421	163.2659	181.9361	4.763193	30	5,172.424
May 1989	185.0094	7.053769	175.298	195.1131	5.055306	31	5,735.291
June 1989	208.4441	8.435192	197.6702	219.6464	5.606632	30	6,253.324
July 1989	233.8093	9.9547	221.8878	246.1981	6.202092	31	7,248.089
August 1989	301.4719	17.27481	286.1594	317.3822	7.965613	31	9,345.63
September 1989	382.7725	32.15915	362.5492	403.8182	10.52868	30	11,483.17
October 2005	295.6721	35.55362	278.482	313.6348	8.96845	31	9,165.836
November 2005	261.663	30.30842	246.0415	278.0063	8.155171	30	7,849.89
December 2005	199.3194	18.11428	187.4598	211.7251	6.190786	31	6,178.902
January 2006	203.9594	18.51091	191.8827	216.5894	6.303389	31	6,322.742
February 2006	272.5295	34.30058	255.5499	290.3296	8.873419	28	7,630.827
March 2006	244.9012	26.42326	230.2263	260.2568	7.661655	31	7,591.937
April 2006	135.5957	6.732651	127.7419	143.801	4.0971	30	4,067.87
May 2006	145.5025	7.182253	137.226	154.1424	4.315819	31	4,510.576
June 2006	163.9336	8.589132	154.7702	173.4922	4.776467	30	4,918.008
July 2006	183.8822	10.45142	173.7128	194.4855	5.299647	31	5,700.349
August 2006	237.0942	18.81622	223.8884	250.8676	6.883076	31	7,349.921
September 2006	301.0293	35.53325	283.4427	319.4102	9.17633	30	9,030.878
			Annual loads				
Water year 1989	279.8538	7.436798	273.3776	286.4427	3.332978	365	102,146.6
Water year 2006	220.0486	12.68671	212.5653	227.725	3.8674	365	80,317.74

[1] Raw output data from S-LOADEST (Insightful Corp., 2005a), not adjusted to significant figures.

Table 15.   S-LOADEST salinity load output[1] for site 6 from water year 1982 to water year 2006.

[Flux, salinity load in tons per day; Variance, the variability of flux in tons per day; Lower 95, lower limit of the 95th percentile confidence interval; Upper 95, upper limit of the 95th percentile confidence interval; SEP, standard error of flux prediction, in tons per day; N, number of days; Load, salinity load in tons per month]

Date	Flux	Variance	Lower 95	Upper 95	SEP	N	Load
			Monthly loads				
October 1981	60.75667	3.723138	55.6944	66.1515	2.668193	31	1,883.457
November 1981	32.35392	1.016975	29.69148	35.18897	1.40271	30	970.6177
December 1981	32.56373	1.039239	29.89949	35.39961	1.403379	31	1,009.476
January 1982	32.6166	1.022836	29.96268	35.44051	1.39769	31	1,011.115
February 1982	38.36821	1.384513	35.17827	41.76722	1.68121	28	1,074.31
March 1982	38.2338	1.341957	35.14141	41.52301	1.628282	31	1,185.248
April 1982	31.96629	0.941498	29.37342	34.72468	1.365392	30	958.9886
May 1982	68.62837	4.44333	62.98947	74.63223	2.970702	31	2,127.479
June 1982	81.65951	6.233324	75.03049	88.71209	3.490906	30	2,449.785
July 1982	80.3222	5.667588	73.94957	87.0922	3.353353	31	2,489.988
August 1982	81.23555	6.064487	74.71902	88.16322	3.430315	31	2,518.302
September 1982	80.95409	6.74875	74.20178	88.15047	3.559093	30	2,428.623
October 2005	38.54942	1.935221	35.11001	42.23191	1.817256	31	1,195.032
November 2005	20.52818	0.53376	18.71563	22.46742	0.957318	30	615.8455
December 2005	20.66208	0.511987	18.87795	22.56796	0.941544	31	640.5245
January 2006	20.69643	0.47258	18.95074	22.5583	0.920497	31	641.5893
February 2006	24.34688	0.600275	22.28626	26.54516	1.086693	28	681.7127
March 2006	24.26184	0.570828	22.27263	26.3795	1.047887	31	752.117
April 2006	20.28433	0.415058	18.60136	22.07736	0.886922	30	608.5299
May 2006	43.54839	1.955952	39.88996	47.44926	1.928807	31	1,350
June 2006	51.81562	2.924937	47.4408	56.48192	2.306913	30	1,554.469
July 2006	50.96475	2.918861	46.65539	55.56168	2.272508	31	1,579.907
August 2006	51.54253	3.274258	47.07118	56.32053	2.36007	31	1,597.818
September 2006	51.36311	3.629706	46.7245	56.33384	2.451976	30	1,540.893
			Annual loads				
Water year 1982	55.08874	0.998839	52.92079	57.32168	1.122728	365	20,107.39
Water year 2006	34.95463	0.659056	33.27217	36.69921	0.874305	365	12,758.44

[1] Raw output data from S-LOADEST (Insightful Corp., 2005a), not adjusted to significant figures.

Table 16.   S-LOADEST salinity load output[1] for site 6 from water year 1990 to water year 2006.

[Flux, salinity load in tons per day; Variance, the variability of flux in tons per day; Lower 95, lower limit of the 95th percentile confidence interval; Upper 95, upper limit of the 95th percentile confidence interval; SEP, standard error of flux prediction, in tons per day; N, number of days; Load, salinity load in tons per month]

Date	Flux	Variance	Lower 95	Upper 95	SEP	N	Load
			Monthly loads				
October 1989	51.39102	2.425028	47.18037	55.87337	2.218055	31	1,593.122
November 1989	24.06166	0.530443	22.09838	26.15107	1.034059	30	721.8499
December 1989	20.85432	0.413105	19.16499	22.65135	0.889556	31	646.484
January 1990	24.73121	0.517532	22.76701	26.81801	1.033616	31	766.6674
February 1990	26.47705	0.563978	24.35367	28.73435	1.11774	28	741.3574
March 1990	24.07694	0.466386	22.14692	26.12864	1.015942	31	746.3853
April 1990	23.56537	0.458874	21.70043	25.54628	0.981272	30	706.961
May 1990	58.42862	2.686399	53.8158	63.32757	2.426932	31	1,811.287
June 1990	67.27927	3.5265	62.04629	72.83175	2.7519	30	2,018.378
July 1990	66.53299	3.33994	61.43959	71.93216	2.677153	31	2,062.523
August 1990	65.99597	3.501298	60.8712	71.43309	2.694852	31	2,045.875
September 1990	68.90015	4.527589	63.24835	74.91709	2.977329	30	2,067.005
October 2005	38.40664	1.851289	34.99682	42.05618	1.801292	31	1,190.606
November 2005	17.9822	0.407868	16.38838	19.68788	0.841912	30	539.4661
December 2005	15.58554	0.304892	14.22475	17.04031	0.718424	31	483.1519
January 2006	18.48351	0.37256	16.91954	20.15191	0.824766	31	572.9887
February 2006	19.78868	0.396019	18.11514	21.5739	0.88253	28	554.0829
March 2006	17.99496	0.324046	16.47768	19.61318	0.800048	31	557.8437
April 2006	17.61246	0.322287	16.13839	19.18383	0.777063	30	528.3739
May 2006	43.66899	1.891992	40.02872	47.54852	1.918724	31	1,353.739
June 2006	50.28277	2.600492	46.09964	54.74025	2.204702	30	1,508.483
July 2006	49.72358	2.625428	45.58283	54.13619	2.182443	31	1,541.431
August 2006	49.32114	2.811982	45.11926	53.80568	2.216417	31	1,528.955
September 2006	51.49108	3.510562	46.8817	56.42738	2.435719	30	1,544.732
			Annual loads				
Water year 2006	43.63807	0.403237	42.16735	45.14638	0.759981	365	15,927.89
Water year 2006	32.6133	0.533049	31.08463	34.19687	0.793991	365	11,903.85

[1] Raw output data from S-LOADEST (Insightful Corp , 2005a), not adjusted to significant figures.

Table 17.   S-LOADEST salinity load output[1] for site 17 from water year 1978 to water year 2006.

[Flux, salinity load in tons per day; Variance, the variability of flux in tons per day; Lower 95, lower limit of the 95th percentile confidence interval; Upper 95, upper limit of the 95th percentile confidence interval; SEP, standard error of flux prediction, in tons per day; N, number of days; Load, salinity load in tons per month]

Date	Flux	Variance	Lower 95	Upper 95	SEP	N	Load
			Monthly loads				
October 1977	40.26557	0.893911	37.67356	42.9872	1.355689	31	1,248.233
November 1977	46.94168	1.464416	43.74402	50.30904	1.674984	30	1,408.25
December 1977	115.8907	18.47344	106.0259	126.4184	5.203315	31	3,592.61
January 1978	376.9504	340.4961	337.903	419.2389	20.75588	31	11,685.46
February 1978	688.7389	1106.822	617.9387	765.3672	37.62166	28	19,284.69
March 1978	507.1954	298.5532	466.6068	550.3383	21.36426	31	15,723.06
April 1978	184.6291	18.55128	172.5368	197.3372	6.327431	30	5,538.874
May 1978	129.2057	16.21848	119.5045	139.4774	5.095981	31	4,005.376
June 1978	92.58728	11.89331	84.7361	100.964	4.140674	30	2,777.618
July 1978	64.73419	6.215376	59.15195	70.69682	2.94579	31	2,006.76
August 1978	50.31959	2.828318	46.37349	54.50872	2.075701	31	1,559.907
September 1978	40.27198	1.182284	37.46813	43.22808	1.469589	30	1,208.159
October 2005	35.28861	0.973668	32.80276	37.91112	1.303346	31	1,093.947
November 2005	41.13781	1.655952	38.01882	44.44215	1.638892	30	1,234.134
December 2005	101.5562	18.59494	92.07178	111.7447	5.019941	31	3,148.243
January 2006	330.3138	316.1743	293.4992	370.4372	19.63467	31	10,239.73
February 2006	603.5405	1016.827	537.1106	675.8602	35.40869	28	16,899.14
March 2006	444.4913	286.5365	406.2222	485.3639	20.1938	31	13,779.23
April 2006	161.8248	14.94537	151.1103	173.0911	5.608084	30	4,854.744
May 2006	113.2532	11.38591	104.9753	122.0042	4.344809	31	3,510.848
June 2006	81.15684	8.431544	74.45584	88.29379	3.530823	30	2,434.705
July 2006	56.7411	4.574324	51.91991	61.88569	2.542853	31	1,758.974
August 2006	44.1039	2.268065	40.59736	47.8296	1.845314	31	1,367.221
September 2006	35.29524	1.122912	32.68814	38.05304	1.368823	30	1,058.857
			Annual loads				
Water year 1978	191.8877	29.93164	180.7276	203.5495	5.822514	365	70,039.00
Water year 2006	168.1637	31.52441	156.9326	179.9787	5.879899	365	61,379.77

[1] Raw output data from S-LOADEST (Insightful Corp , 2005a), not adjusted to significant figures

Table 18. S-LOADEST salinity load output[1] for site 17 from water year 1989 to water year 2006.

[Flux, salinity load in tons per day; Variance, the variability of flux in tons per day; Lower 95, lower limit of the 95th percentile confidence interval; Upper 95, upper limit of the 95th percentile confidence interval; SEP, standard error of flux prediction, in tons per day; N, number of days; Load, salinity load in tons per month]

Date	Flux	Variance	Lower 95	Upper 95	SEP	N	Load
			Monthly loads				
October 1988	63.67971	1.880746	59.72558	67.82421	2.066215	31	1,974.071
November 1988	50.02361	1.256015	46.8426	53.36166	1.663227	30	1,500.708
December 1988	40.83264	0.876981	38.23111	43.56286	1.360306	31	1,265.812
January 1989	38.96551	0.766695	36.50767	41.54365	1.284842	31	1,207.931
February 1989	42.43196	0.83544	39.72623	45.27165	1.414821	28	1,188.095
March 1989	101.0474	4.692727	94.57737	107.8392	3.383538	31	3,132.47
April 1989	271.0859	43.07007	252.9064	290.2144	9.51863	30	8,132.577
May 1989	496.9017	158.9303	463.5512	531.9945	17.4624	31	15,403.95
June 1989	326.3516	43.96826	306.1186	347.5572	10.57231	30	9,790.549
July 1989	126.4145	8.715746	118.2241	135.0172	4.284507	31	3,918.849
August 1989	98.88905	5.331119	92.53792	105.557	3.3216	31	3,065.561
September 1989	84.46043	3.32377	79.15704	90.02216	2.772042	30	2,533.813
October 2005	58.7427	2.82372	54.5415	63.17859	2.20368	31	1,821.024
November 2005	46.15409	1.928937	42.73938	49.76652	1.792936	30	1,384.623
December 2005	37.68167	1.332416	34.88203	40.64416	1.470177	31	1,168.132
January 2006	35.96156	1.149699	33.33347	38.73986	1.379405	31	1,114.808
February 2006	39.1619	1.212681	36.33113	42.1526	1.485303	28	1,096.533
March 2006	93.26071	6.725166	86.52773	100.3736	3.532661	31	2,891.082
April 2006	250.1963	56.20576	231.4746	270.0151	9.833431	30	7,505.888
May 2006	458.6128	199.1639	424.3654	494.8628	17.98708	31	14,217
June 2006	301.2127	60.02985	280.4987	323.037	10.85317	30	9,036.381
July 2006	116.6801	10.0423	108.5289	125.2754	4.27269	31	3,617.082
August 2006	91.27183	6.57373	84.82389	98.07535	3.380985	31	2,829.427
September 2006	77.95150	4.801134	72.38793	83.82519	2.918117	30	2,338.545
			Annual loads				
Water year 1989	145.5189	4.114463	140.7056	150.4529	2.486641	365	53,114.39
Water year 2006	134.3028	8.807987	128.0426	140.7865	3.251208	365	49,020.52

[1] Raw output data from S-LOADEST (Insightful Corp., 2005a), not adjusted to significant figures.